THE PREHISTORIC EARTH

THE FIRST VERTEBRATES

OCEANS OF THE PALEOZOIC ERA

THE PREHISTORIC EARTH

THE PREHISTORIC EARTH

THE FIRST VERTEBRATES

OCEANS OF THE PALEOZOIC ERA

Thom Holmes

CHELSEA HOUSE
PUBLISHERS
An imprint of Infobase Publishing

THE PREHISTORIC EARTH: The First Vertebrates

Copyright © 2008 by Infobase Publishing

Chelsea House
An imprint of Infobase Publishing
132 West 31st Street
New York NY 10001

Library of Congress Cataloging-in-Publication Data

Holmes, Thom.
  The first vertebrates / Thom Holmes.
    p. cm. — (The prehistoric Earth)
  Includes bibliographical references and index.
  ISBN 978-0-8160-5958-4 (hardcover)
  1. Fishes, Fossil—Study and teaching—United States. 2. Geology, Stratigraphic—Paleozoic.
I. Title. II. Series.

  QE851.H65 2008
  567—dc22   2007045329

Text design by Kerry Casey
Cover design by Salvatore Luongo

Printed in the United States of America

Bang NMSG 10 9 8 7 6 5 4 3 2 1

This book is printed on acid-free paper.

Contents

PREFACE

To be curious about the future, one must know something about the past.

Humans have been recording events in the world around them for about 5,300 years. That is how long it has been since the Sumerian people, in a land that today is southern Iraq, invented the first known written language. Writing allowed people to document what they saw happening around them. The written word gave a new permanency to life. Language, and writing in particular, made history possible.

History is a marvelous human invention, but how do people know about things that happened before language existed? Or before humans existed? Events that took place before human record keeping began are called *prehistory*. Prehistoric life is, by its definition, any life that existed before human beings existed and were able to record for posterity what was happening in the world around them.

Prehistory is as much a product of the human mind as history. Scientists who specialize in unraveling clues of prehistoric life are called *paleontologists*. They study life that existed before human history, often hundreds of thousands and millions of years in the past. Their primary clues come from fossils of animals and plants and from geologic evidence about Earth's topography and climate. Through the skilled and often imaginative interpretation of fossils, paleontologists are able to reconstruct the appearance, lifestyle, environment, and relationships of ancient life-forms. While paleontology is grounded in a study of prehistoric life, it draws on many other sciences to complete an accurate picture of the past. Information from the fields of biology, zoology, geology, chemistry, meteorology, and even astrophysics is called into play to help the paleontologist view the past through the lens of today's knowledge.

6

If a writer were to write a history of all sports, would it be enough to write only about table tennis? Certainly not. On the shelves of bookstores and libraries, however, we find just such a slanted perspective toward the story of the dinosaurs. Dinosaurs have captured our imagination at the expense of many other equally fascinating, terrifying, and unusual creatures. Dinosaurs were not alone in the pantheon of prehistoric life, but it is rare to find a book that also mentions the many other kinds of life that came before and after the dinosaurs.

The Prehistoric Earth is a series that explores the evolution of life from its earliest forms 3.5 billion years ago until the emergence of modern humans some 300,000 years ago. Four volumes in the series trace the story of the dinosaurs. Six other volumes are devoted to the kinds of animals that evolved before, during, and after the reign of the dinosaurs. *The Prehistoric Earth* covers the early explosion of life in the oceans; the invasion of the land by the first land animals; the rise of fishes, amphibians, reptiles, mammals, and birds; and the emergence of modern humans.

The Prehistoric Earth series is written for readers in high school. Based on the latest scientific findings in paleontology, *The Prehistoric Earth* is the most comprehensive and up-to-date series of its kind for this age group.

EXPLORING PAST LIFE

The language of science is used throughout this series, with ample definition and with an extensive glossary provided in each volume. Important concepts involving geology, evolution, and the lifestyles of early animals are presented logically, step by step. Illustrations, photographs, tables, and maps reinforce and enhance the books' presentation of the story of prehistoric life.

While telling the story of prehistoric life, the author hopes that many readers will be sufficiently intrigued to continue studies on their own. For this purpose, throughout each volume, special "Think About It" sidebars offer additional insights or interesting exercises for readers who wish to explore certain topics. Each book in the series also provides a chapter-by-chapter bibliography of books, journals, and Web sites.

Only about one-tenth of 1 percent of all species of prehistoric animals are known from fossils. A multitude of discoveries remain to be made in the field of paleontology. It is with earnest, best wishes that I hope that some of these discoveries will be made by readers inspired by this series.

—Thom Holmes
Jersey City, New Jersey

ACKNOWLEDGMENTS

I would like to thank the many dedicated and hardworking people at Chelsea House. A special debt of gratitude goes to my editors, Shirley White, Brian Belval, and Frank Darmstadt, for their support and guidance in conceiving and making *The Prehistoric Earth* a reality. Frank and Brian were instrumental in fine-tuning the features of the series as well as accepting my ambitious plan for creating a comprehensive reference for students. Brian greatly influenced the development of the color illustration program and supported my efforts to integrate the work of some of the best artists in the field, most notably John Sibbick, whose work appears throughout the set. Shirley's excellent questions about the science behind the books contributed greatly to the readability of the result.

I am privileged to have worked with some of the brightest minds in paleontology on this series. Ted Daeschler of the Academy of Natural Sciences in Philadelphia reviewed the draft of *The First Vertebrates* and made many important suggestions that affected the course of the work. Ted also wrote the Foreword for the volume.

The excellent copyediting of Mary Ellen Kelly was both thoughtful and vital to shaping the final manuscript. I thank Mary Ellen for her valuable review and suggestions that help make the books a success.

In many ways, a set of books such as this requires years of preparation. Some of the work is educational, and I owe much gratitude to Dr. Peter Dodson of the University of Pennsylvania for his gracious and inspiring tutelage over the years. Another dimension of preparation requires experience digging fossils, and for giving me these opportunities I thank my friends and colleagues who have taken me into the field with them, including Phil Currie, Rodolfo Coria, Matthew Lammana, and Ruben Martinez. Finally comes the work

9

needed to put thoughts down on paper and complete the draft of a book, a process that always takes many more hours than I plan on. I thank Anne for bearing with my constant state of busy-ness and for helping me remember the important things in life. You are an inspiration to me. I also thank my daughter Shaina, the genius in the family and another inspiration, for always being supportive and humoring her father's obsession with prehistoric life.

FOREWORD

The Paleozoic Era witnessed a dramatic and far-reaching revolution in the history of life on Earth. Near the start of the Paleozoic Era, 500 million years ago, backboned animals were no more than small, wriggling ribbons of muscle specialized for life on the sandy shoals of shallow marine ecosystems. By the end of the Paleozoic Era, 250 million years later, vertebrate life had diversified into a wide range of complex forms that filled ecological niches throughout Earth's biosphere. This new diversity of vertebrates included organisms with a wide range of body plans, some of which would survive the test of time and others of which would disappear, leaving fossilized remains but no living descendents in the modern world.

Many people are interested in the wide diversity and seemingly bizarre nature of past life. This volume of Thom Holmes's series *The Prehistoric Earth* delivers a menagerie of early vertebrates and offers a detailed account of the fascinatingly quirky origin of backboned animals and the rise of fish. *The First Vertebrates* provides important lessons in the nature of the evolutionary process as it makes a comprehensive examination of early experimentation with the vertebrate body plan. From today's perspective, life in the Paleozoic oceans may seem strange; but the features that developed in the first vertebrates that lived in those oceans and in their subsequent lineages are crucially important to the history of life. The features of those Paleozoic vertebrates determined the basic design that vertebrate groups would carry forward through evolutionary time.

In *The First Vertebrates,* Thom Holmes sets the stage for the Paleozoic explosion of vertebrate life with a review of the changing physical conditions on Earth during this crucial interval. Continental drift and changing climates had a profound influence on the ecosystems where early vertebrates lived. Sometimes conditions provided stable conditions under which life thrived and diversified; at other times, Earth went through periods of rapid change during which many kinds of life perished in mass extinctions. Several new discoveries discussed in this volume have greatly informed our knowledge of the early stages in the origin of vertebrates. The identification of the conodont and of the details of that animal's anatomy is a particularly interesting example of a detective story in paleontology.

Thom Holmes's survey of the agnathans, or jawless fishes, provides a rare glimpse at these early experiments in free-swimming vertebrates. The variety and nature of the underappreciated agnathans are rarely discussed in popular books, but here you will learn about the dazzling diversity of these primitive vertebrates. Such creatures as ostracoderms, heterostracans, and anaspids probably are not the stuff of Hollywood movies, but for their place in the history of vertebrate life, they deserve the attention that Holmes gives them.

By the Late Ordovician Epoch, the first jawed vertebrates made their appearance, and a new phase of evolutionary experimentation began. A wide range of novel ecological opportunities for fish were made manifest in the evolution of new features in both predators and their prey. Acanthodians and placoderms are two fascinating groups of jawed vertebrates that became quite diverse for a time, particularly during the Devonian Period, but that ultimately did not persist beyond the Paleozoic Era. These forms lived alongside early examples of cartilaginous and bony fish, groups that would endure through time and diversify into the great variety of fish and limbed vertebrates that we know today.

Some of the Paleozoic sharks discussed in *The First Vertebrates* have amazing features: a huge whorl of sharp teeth protruding from the chin in *Helicoprion*, for example, and a brushlike dorsal-fin appendage in *Stethacanthus*. Thom Holmes clearly delights in these creatures and certainly enjoys bringing them to the attention of his readers.

The bony fishes, which are divided into ray-finned and lobe-finned groups, round out the cast of characters in *The First Vertebrates*. As usual, Holmes provides an up-to-date review of these important lineages and includes the latest discoveries.

Evolutionary change in vertebrates is always constrained by the fundamental design features of the vertebrate body, many of which were first established in Paleozoic fish. *The First Vertebrates* provides a firm foundation for understanding the great profusion of fish, amphibians, reptiles, birds, and mammals that derived from Paleozoic fish. It is no exaggeration to say that we can trace the origin of some of the basic traits of our own bodies back to creatures that swam in the watery cradle of the Paleozoic oceans.

—Ted Daeschler
Academy of Natural Sciences, Philadelphia
June 2006

INTRODUCTION

The **Cambrian Period**—the first of the Paleozoic Era—was notable for its remarkable explosion of multicelled **organisms** with hard parts such as shells and **exoskeletons**. The Cambrian saw the beginning of an escalating confrontation between **predator** and prey. An explosion of diverse life-forms during the Cambrian laid the foundation for all major animal **phyla** that exist today. Yet as remarkable as it was, life during the Cambrian Period was only the beginning of a biological drama that would extend for another 237 million years of the Paleozoic Era.

The First Vertebrates begins the story of the vertebrates, some of the most familiar of all animals. Humans are just one of about 45,000 living **species** of vertebrates. The prehistoric past was populated by hundreds of thousands of vertebrate species (now extinct)—only a fraction of which are currently understood from the **fossil** record. Vertebrates of one form or another—beginning with the fishes and extending through amphibians, reptiles, dinosaurs, birds, and mammals—have played an important role in ecological niches worldwide for nearly every time span of their existence.

The denizens of the Paleozoic oceans are the subject of *The First Vertebrates*. They are the first players in the unfolding drama of marine and terrestrial vertebrate **evolution** that occupies the stage throughout the rest of the saga of *The Prehistoric Earth*.

OVERVIEW OF *THE FIRST VERTEBRATES*

The rise of the first vertebrates is synonymous with the Paleozoic Era. This was a time span of increasing ecological complexity. *The First Vertebrates* begins, in Section 1, with a look at the dramatic geological and climatic conditions of the Paleozoic that made the evolution of vertebrate species possible. Chapter 1 describes widespread changes to ocean and land environments, including worldwide **climate** changes that served as catalysts for the diversification of species. Chapter 2 explains how a series of catastrophic **mass extinctions** changed the direction of evolution several times during the Paleozoic Era, leading to the demise of many species and the rise of others.

Vertebrates are the most popular residents of natural history museums around the world. There is an obvious bias toward the display of big, bony skeletons over the display of the remains of any invertebrate. This bias exists despite the fact that animals with backbones make up less than 5 percent of all known animal species. One reason for the popularity of animals with backbones is that their long evolutionary history can be traced through millions of years of extraordinary fossil preservation. In Section 2 of *The First Vertebrates*, the emphasis shifts to an examination of vertebrates, their origins, and their diverse **taxa**.

The first vertebrates are the stars of Section 2. In Chapter 3, vertebrates are defined by their shared anatomical characteristics—the kinds of clues that **paleontologists** use to identify vertebrate species from the distant past. Chapter 4 offers the early fossil record of vertebrates and recounts the recent discovery of the oldest known vertebrates, dating from the time of the Cambrian explosion of life some 525 million years ago.

The four chapters of Section 3 explore the evolution and diversification of Paleozoic fishes, the first successful groups of vertebrates. A span from the Ordovician Period to the end of the Permian Period—237 million years of fish evolution—is broken down into several key stages. Chapter 5 covers the jawless fishes, which are known for their bony exoskeletons. Chapter 6 investigates the evolution of key anatomical innovations of vertebrates such as jaws, the bony skeleton, and paired fins. Chapter 7 introduces the carilaginous sharks and rays. In Chapter 8, *The First Vertebrates* concludes with an exploration of the most successful group of backboned animals, the bony fishes.

Each chapter uses an abundance of tables, maps, figures, and photos to fully depict the lives, habitats, and changing evolutionary patterns of Paleozoic organisms. Many chapters also include Think About It boxes that elaborate on interesting issues, people, and discoveries related to Paleozoic life.

The First Vertebrates builds on foundational principles of geology, fossils, and the study of life. Perhaps the most important principles to keep in mind as one reads this book are the basic rules governing evolution: that the direction of evolution is determined first by the traits inherited by individuals and then by the interaction of each individual with its habitat as well as random mutations in DNA that make each individual unique. These changes accumulate, generation after generation, and allow species to adapt to changing conditions in the world around them. As Charles Darwin (1809–1882) explained, "The small differences distinguishing varieties of the same species steadily tend to increase, till they equal the greater differences between species of the same genus, or even of distinct genera." These are the rules of nature that drove the engine of evolution during the Paleozoic Era and gave rise to forms of life whose descendants still populate the Earth.

SECTION ONE:
THE WORLD OF THE
PALEOZOIC ERA

Continents and Climates of the Paleozoic Era

The Paleozoic Era stretched back from 251 million to 542 million years ago. It marked the rise of plant and animal species that eventually led to the kinds of life we see in today's world. These formative years were marked by dramatic changes to the geology and climate of Earth—changes that triggered the development of thousands of species of organisms. The struggle for survival and the ability to adapt were played out against a backdrop of radical flux in Earth's habitats. This chapter explores the geological and climatic changes that affected the evolution of life in the Paleozoic Era.

GEOLOGIC TIME PERIODS OF THE PALEOZOIC ERA

The **geologic time scale** is a scale for naming long periods of Earth's past. This time scale consists of a nested hierarchy of time spans of decreasing length, from **eons** and **eras** to **periods** and **epochs**. The lengths of these time spans are based on the geology and paleontology of the Earth layers that mark their beginnings and ends. Some of these layers took longer than others to accumulate, a fact that accounts for the different lengths of the time spans. Many of the major divisions between geologic time spans are also marked by significant events, such as mass extinctions, **glaciation**, and widespread volcanic activity. Such geologic events often mark transitions and extinctions in the fossil record and restrict the remains of given plant and animal species to certain layers.

The organisms described in this book lived during the Paleozoic ("ancient life") Era, a span of time that lasted for 291 million years. The Paleozoic has been divided into six periods, each of which ends with a mass extinction.

PERIODS OF THE PALEOZOIC ERA

Period	Time Span (millions of years ago)	Duration (millions of years)
Permian	251 to 299	48
Carboniferous	299 to 359	60
Devonian	359 to 416	57
Silurian	416 to 443	27
Ordovician	443 to 488	45
Cambrian	488 to 542	54

The Paleozoic world was subject to many natural events that would dramatically affect the history of life. The evolving Earth was experiencing widespread tectonic disruptions, abrupt swings in global temperature, fluctuating sea levels, and fundamental changes to the makeup of the planet's gaseous atmosphere. The era was also marked by long spans of temperate warmth contrasted with the chilling effect of massive glaciations. The Paleozoic Era was a time of extremes that greatly affected the direction that life could take.

CONTINENTAL AND OCEANIC CHANGES: THE ROLE OF PLATE TECTONICS

Earth's surface is made up of many large slabs of **crust** that ride on top of the planet's molten-hot **mantle**. These slabs are called **tectonic plates**. A dozen or more of these plates, located on dry land and beneath the sea, interlock to make up the fragmented crust of the Earth. The individual forces of heat and gravity that change the face of the Earth combine to move the continental plates over long periods of time, a phenomenon called **continental drift**.

The habitats created by the changing face of the Earth served as the stage for the evolution of the organisms that will be discussed in the remaining chapters of this book.

Like tectonic plate movements, changes to the level of the oceans and the formation of ice sheets and polar ice caps are relatively slow geologic processes. They are also intimately connected. During periods of glaciation, ice sheets absorb much of the water in Earth's water budget. When this happens, the sea level can drop around the world, affecting and sometimes wiping out near-shore habitats and eliminating some species of plants and animals in the process.

The extraordinary rearranging of Earth's continents and oceans during the second half of the Paleozoic Era played havoc with the habitats of the world's plants and animals. It is no wonder that the Paleozoic hosted some of the most severe mass extinction events of all time.

GLOBAL TEMPERATURES AND PALEOCLIMATES

The geography of land and sea masses is not the only natural phenomenon that influences the survival and evolution of species. Climate plays an equally vital role in determining the direction that life on Earth can take.

The study of prehistoric climates is known as **paleoclimatology**. Scientists draw on a variety of data sources to determine past climates. Among the leading lines of evidence are the distribution of climate-sensitive plant and animal fossils, the occurrence of certain kinds of rock strata known to be restricted to certain kinds of climates, and a variety of paleoclimate indicators derived from the study of particular natural phenomena. Among those indicators are the examination of tree rings (dendrochronology), the study of the shape and surface area of fossil leaves, and the examination of ice cores, lake sediment, cave deposits, and the oxygen isotope content of marine shells. Evidence derived from such studies can

(continues on page 24)

The Cambrian Period
(542–488 million years ago)

The Ordovician Period
(488–443 million years ago)

The Silurian Period
(443–416 million years ago)

An illustrated guide to continental drift

The Devonian Period
(416–359 million years ago)

The Carboniferous Period
(359–299 million years ago)

The Permian Period
(299–251 million years ago)

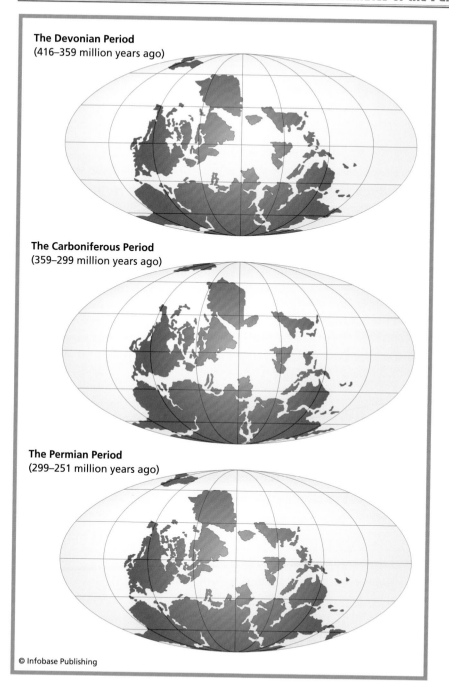

(continued from page 21)

reveal climatic trends such as **average global temperature** and **precipitation**.

Determining the average global temperature of the distant past provides critical clues about the life of the past, especially about the effect of climate changes on ancestors of modern plants and animals whose sensitivity to temperature fluctuations is well understood. Of the available techniques for determining past global temperatures, the use of oxygen isotope readings from marine shells is one of the most reliable. Using a mass spectrometer, scientists can measure the proportions of certain oxygen isotopes in calcium carbonate shells. In the study of modern marine shells, it has been determined that the amount of these isotopes in seawater varies predictably with the temperature of the ocean. By comparing oxygen isotope readings of modern shells to those of prehistoric shells, it is possible to chart likely average global temperatures as far back as the **Precambrian Era**.

Factors Affecting Global Temperature

Average global temperature is regulated by many interrelated factors. These include the output of the Sun, the reflective nature of the Earth, the proximity of the poles to landmasses or oceans, and the ability of solar radiation to penetrate the atmosphere. Together, these factors determine how much solar radiation is absorbed or reflected by the Earth, resulting in a ratio called the **global heat budget**. The global heat budget is governed by the following principles.

Incoming radiation from the Sun. The Sun provides a reliable bombardment of solar radiation. Earth has never experienced a serious fluctuation in the Sun's radiation output that would drastically alter average global temperature. Scientists must, therefore, turn to other factors, all of them earthbound, that might affect the global heat budget.

Reflectivity of Earth's surface. Landmasses retain far less heat than water. Seawater in particular plays a key role in regulating the global thermometer. Oceans not only absorb heat, but they also distribute it widely across the planet through ocean currents. What we can deduce from this is that the planet will be warmer when the ratio of ocean to land surface is greater, and cooler when the reverse is true.

REFLECTIVITY OF EARTH SURFACES AFFECTING THE GLOBAL HEAT BUDGET

Surface Type	Reflectivity (Percentage of Solar Radiation Reflected)
Water	2–8%
Dark-colored rocks and forests	5–10%
Light-colored rocks and barren ground	15–20%
Grasslands	15–35%
Atmosphere (clouds and dust)	40–80%
Snow and ice	45–85%

Proximity of the poles to oceans and landmasses. Earth's poles have not always been landlocked or nearly landlocked as they are today. Oceans of the polar regions absorb heat from the Sun more quickly than polar landmasses and ice caps. That is because the snowy surface of the frozen earth reflects most of the sunlight that falls upon it. A polar region can be significantly warmer if it consists of more ocean than land. The temperature of the polar regions in turn affects the circulation of atmospheric temperature across the planet. Colder poles can cause a drop in average global temperature.

Ability of solar radiation to penetrate the atmosphere. Clouds and debris such as smoke, dust, and airborne chemicals are effective deflectors of solar radiation. The global heat budget can be greatly affected by temporary increases in atmospheric debris. It is estimated that an increase in atmospheric smoke and dirt of only seven percent for one year could drop the average global temperature by 2°F (1°C). In one modern example, the 1991 eruption of Mount Pinatubo in the Philippines discharged an enormous amount of ash and sulfur dioxide into the atmosphere. When sulfur dioxide is combined with water vapor in clouds, it creates a radiation-absorbing shield of sulfuric acid vapor. Using evidence collected by satellite, NASA scientists confirmed that the eruption of Mount Pinatubo caused a drop in average global temperature of 1°F (0.5°C). This suggests that times of massive volcanic activity such as occurred during part of the Paleozoic Era may have contributed to lowering global temperatures enough to encourage glaciation.

Ability of the atmosphere to trap reflected radiation. If all of the Sun's radiation reflected from Earth's surface bounced back through the atmosphere into space, the planet would be a cold, uninhabitable place. Some of this reflected radiation is prevented from escaping by water vapor in clouds, ozone in the lower atmosphere, and atmospheric methane and carbon dioxide (CO_2) gas. The trapping of this radiation is called the **greenhouse effect**. When the amounts of these atmospheric chemicals are increased, more heat is trapped, and the planet grows warmer. This may be happening now, in the twenty-first century, as a result of humans burning fossil fuels such as wood, coal, and petroleum. A byproduct of fossil fuel consumption is the release of carbon dioxide into the air. In Earth's past, the opposite effect occurred during times when atmospheric carbon dioxide was absorbed by carbon-rich sediments such as limestone and coal deposits. Chemical studies of glacial ice cores have confirmed that atmospheric carbon dioxide was much lower during past glacial episodes. This suggests that a lowering of CO_2 in the atmosphere may have preceded periods of glaciation.

Of the above factors, the configuration of Earth's land and water surface areas appears to carry the greatest weight in regulating average global temperature. The other factors, although important components of the global heat budget, do not appear to exert extraordinary influence by themselves. If this were not the case, we might expect to see wider fluctuations in the global temperatures of the past. On the contrary, the geologic past shows that Earth has maintained a stable thermal balance that has varied only within a narrow range. Even a renewal of continental glaciation requires a drop in mean annual temperature of only 5° to 9°F (3° to 5°C) to get the cycle started. Most of the planet's geologic history has supported a remarkably stable thermal equilibrium.

Average Global Temperatures of the Paleozoic

With the exception of two periods of glacial cooling, the Paleozoic was a uniformly warm era. For 75 percent of the Paleozoic, average global temperatures ranged between 63° and 72°F (17° and 22°C), with a climate across the world that was much like the climate that exists today along the equator. Even the coolest of Paleozoic times, equal to 25 percent of the entire era, were not extraordinarily cold; those times had an average temperature that ranged between 54° and 63°F (12° and 17°C)—a temperate climate by today's standards. Today's Earth is experiencing a cool period in its geologic history, with an average global temperature that hovers around 54°F (12°C). According to geologists, modern-day Earth currently is experiencing an interglacial period of receding ice sheets that began about 10,000 years ago. The rate of global warming due to human activity on the planet is causing a faster-than-normal rise in average global temperature.

From the Early Cambrian Epoch to the Early Ordovician Epoch, Earth had a mild climate. Warm, tropical oceans and seaways flowed between the southern continent of Gondwana and the fragmented landmasses of the Northern Hemisphere. During the Middle and Late Ordovician Epochs, the world cooled down for a short span; glaciers and an ice cap formed on Gondwana and at the South Pole. During the Silurian Epoch and Early Devonian Epoch, the northern continents became partly arid and desertlike, while cool oceans covered what is today Africa and South America in the Southern Hemisphere.

During the Late Devonian and Early Carboniferous Epochs, the continents of the Northern and Southern Hemispheres slowly began to collide in the early stages of the formation of the supercontinent Pangaea, and distinctive climate zones began to form. The Northern Hemisphere was warm and tropical, with a proliferation of

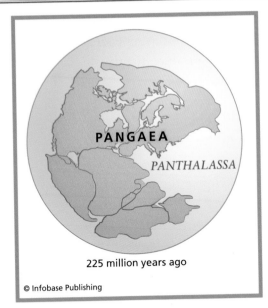

225 million years ago

© Infobase Publishing

The great ocean called Panthalassa surrounded the supercontinent of Pangaea.

rain-forest flora and **fauna**. The South Pole cooled again, glaciers formed, and the area had an ice cap by the Late Carboniferous Epoch. The Early Permian witnessed another period of glaciation, although shorter than that of the Late Ordovician.

The end of the Paleozoic Era witnessed a transformative reversal of climate conditions, as glaciers disappeared from the Southern Hemisphere, and an ice cap formed on the North Pole. Pangaea was now a substantial landmass that included most of Earth's terrestrial environments. Central Pangaea became arid across most of the equator. Only two substantial tropical zones remained, near the equator in what today is southern China, northern Africa, and northern South America. A single great ocean called Panthalassa surrounded the supercontinent Pangaea. The world had six distinctive climate zones: glacial, temperate, semiarid, arid, equatorial-tropical, and equatorial-mountainous.

Oxygen and Carbon Dioxide Levels

Life on land and in water requires carbon dioxide (CO_2) and oxygen (O_2). Plants need carbon dioxide for **photosynthesis**. Carbon dioxide comes from animals when they exhale and from decaying organic matter and is absorbed by water in the atmosphere. This exchange between living organisms and the environment is a critical factor that affects the development of all life. Nearly all types of organisms use oxygen to obtain energy from organic compounds. Oxygen is an essential fuel for body tissues.

Before the evolution of the first single-celled organisms, Earth's atmosphere contained no free oxygen; it consisted primarily of carbon dioxide and nitrogen gas. About 3.5 billion years ago, single-celled cyanobacteria found a niche for themselves by using energy from the Sun, carbon dioxide, and water to reproduce their cells. The waste product of this process was free oxygen; that oxygen was released into the sea and atmosphere, making cyanobacteria the first photosynthetic creatures.

The process of photosynthesis, used by plants, is the major source of atmospheric oxygen. Photosynthesis is also the basis for the essential exchange of chemicals that takes place between plants and animals. Plants consume carbon dioxide and release oxygen; animal respiration consumes oxygen and releases carbon dioxide.

The oceans are part of a complex exchange of life-supporting elements. Under normal conditions, oxygen and carbon dioxide from marine plants, animals, and the atmosphere dissolve in seawater in a proportion equal to that found in the atmosphere. Seawater has the ability to absorb carbon dioxide, making the ocean a vast reservoir of this vital molecule. If seawater becomes depleted of an important element, it draws more of that element from the solid earth or from sediments where chemicals are stored naturally. Carbon dioxide, in turn, helps regulate the pH range of seawater: The CO_2 acts as a check to keep the ocean from becoming too alkaline or too acid, thus maintaining the chemical components of seawater at an optimum level to support life in the ocean. Through these processes, the chemical balance between the oceans and the atmosphere remains in equilibrium.

Oxygen can be added to the ocean only through absorption at the surface or as a byproduct of photosynthesizing marine plants. Concentrations of oxygen adequate to support ocean life can reach depths of 2,600 feet (800 meters) or more through the circulation of ocean currents, although mostly enriching shallower ocean depths.

In the early history of the Earth, the availability of oxygen meant that life, as we understand it, could exist. The explosion of life in the sea and the rise of marine and land vertebrates were synchronous with the increasing abundance of oxygen in the Precambrian and Paleozoic Eras. The first photosynthesizing creatures were the

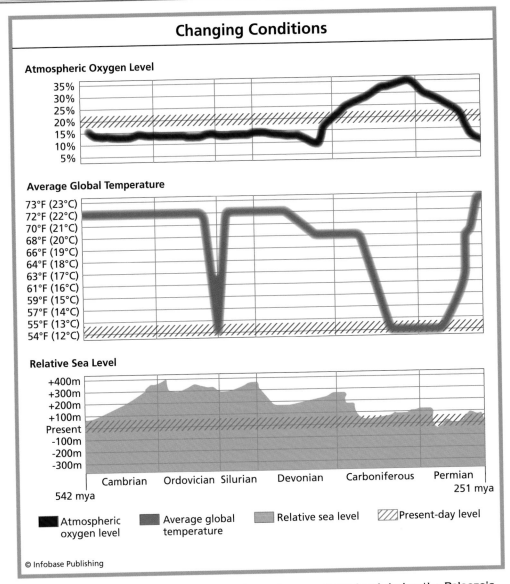

Changing Conditions

Atmospheric Oxygen Level

Average Global Temperature

Relative Sea Level

Cambrian   Ordovician   Silurian   Devonian   Carboniferous   Permian

542 mya

251 mya

■ Atmospheric oxygen level   ■ Average global temperature   ■ Relative sea level   ▨ Present-day level

These graphs show changes to climate, atmosphere, and sea level during the Paleozoic Era. Extreme rises and falls correspond with mass extinction events.

cyanobacteria, which originated about 3.5 billion years ago. By the Early Paleozoic Era, the oxygenation of the oceans led to the rapid development of multicelled organisms. By the middle of the

THINK ABOUT IT

Changing Paleozoic Ecosystems and the Diversification of Organisms

The combined effects of changes in geology and changes in climate have a ripple effect on Earth's marine habitats. During the Early Cambrian Epoch, rising seas spread out to form immense expanses of shallow water across the surface of the continents. With rising oxygen levels, invertebrate life in the oceans grew and diversified rapidly. During the Late Cambrian and Early Ordovician Epochs, sea levels retreated and then rose again; temperatures cooled; and marine habitats became increasingly tiered. There were more and varied places for sea life to live.

The shelled, bottom-dwelling, and crawling creatures that dominated the Cambrian Period were gradually replaced during the Ordovician by a diverse collection of swimmers, stationary filter feeders, drifters, and burrowing creatures that occupied every level of habitat in the ocean. These Ordovician organisms are typified by corals, swimming cephalopods, brachiopods, bryozoans, and plantlike crinoids.

During the Silurian and Devonian Periods, invertebrate life on the seafloor diversified even further, occupying extensive reef habitats in shallow seaways that ran along continental margins. Ammonoids and fishes were widespread during the Devonian Period. On land, the first vascular plants were diversifying into forests, and a wide assortment of terrestrial arthropods became the first important animals to invade the land.

During the Carboniferous Period, great tropical forests spread across a wide equatorial band around Earth, and vertebrates began to inhabit the land. In the oceans, ammonoids, mollusks, crinoids, bryozoans, corals, and fishes were abundant.

By the end of the Paleozoic Era, cyclic drops in sea level and fluctuating temperatures on land and sea were capped by a catastrophic period of volcanic eruptions and runaway greenhouse warming that led to the worst mass extinction event in history.

Paleozoic Era, oxygen levels in the atmosphere rose accordingly, fed by an increasing abundance of plants on both land and sea. During the Carboniferous Period, an enormous greening of the land took place, as vast tropical rain forests spread throughout the hot zones of Earth's equatorial regions. These same regions, now located in North America, Europe, and Asia, still contain the vast coal reserves—the fossilized remains of plants and animals from the Paleozoic Era— that helped fuel humankind's first great industrial revolution.

Oxygen currently makes up about 21 percent of Earth's atmosphere. During the Late Carboniferous Epoch, atmospheric oxygen levels peaked at an astounding 35 percent—a phenomenon that resulted in some unusual animal evolution, including gigantism in insects and other **arthropods**. The combined effects of rising oxygen levels, warming global temperatures, continental drift, and changes in sea level made the Paleozoic Era a time of explosive geologic and biological evolution.

LIFE DIVERSIFIES

The changes of Earth's geology, oceans, and climate during the 291 million years of the Paleozoic Era made possible a growing diversity of organisms on land and sea. Substantial movements of the continents formed entirely new ecological niches. The first explosion of life in the Cambrian seas was followed during the rest of the Paleozoic Era by an ever-widening variety of shelled marine creatures. The first fish evolved during the Cambrian Period and diversified during the Middle Paleozoic Epoch. An increasingly inviting terrestrial environment first drew **bacteria** and then plants to the land, followed soon by arthropods and amphibians. The greening of the continents with vast tropical forests forever changed the ecology of Earth as the processes of weathering, **erosion**, and sedimentation began to transform what was once a barren planet into an inviting world for many kinds of organisms.

While the Paleozoic Era is known for the development of new habitats and an explosion of species, it is also notorious for having hosted some of the worst mass extinction events of all time. This era

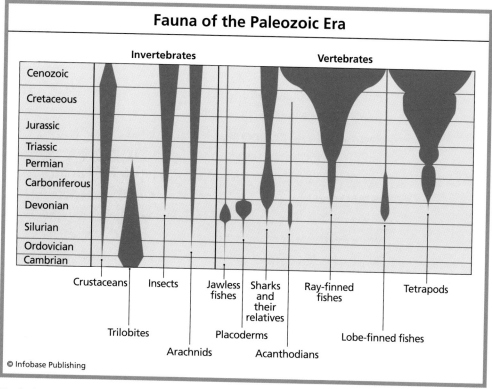

Evolution of major marine and terrestrial organisms during the Paleozoic Era

serves as a reminder that nothing in geologic history is guaranteed, even the survival of a successful species.

SUMMARY

This chapter explored the geological and climatic changes that affected the evolution of life in the Paleozoic Era.

1. The Paleozoic Era stretched back from 251 million to 542 million years ago and marked the rise of plant and animal species that eventually led to the kinds of life we see today.

2. During the first half of the Paleozoic Era, which included the Cambrian, Ordovician, and Silurian Periods, the Earth was a world that consisted of the large southern landmass Gondwana and warm oceans in the Northern Hemisphere.

3. During the second half of the Paleozoic Era, which included the Devonian, Carboniferous, and Permian Periods, all of Earth's major landmasses slowly collided to form the super-continent Pangaea.

4. Pangaea was surrounded by a single great ocean called Panthalassa.

5. Average global temperature is regulated by several interrelated factors, including the output of the Sun, the reflective nature of Earth, the proximity of the poles to landmasses or ocean, and the ability of solar radiation to penetrate Earth's atmosphere. The combined influence of these elements regulates Earth's global heat budget.

6. With the exception of two periods of glacial cooling, the Paleozoic Era was a uniformly warm era.

7. The explosion of life in the sea and the rise of marine and land vertebrates were synchronous with the increasing abundance of oxygen in the Precambrian and Paleozoic Eras.

2

PALEOZOIC MASS EXTINCTIONS

The fossil record confirms the fact that no species lasts forever. Every species eventually becomes extinct. **Extinction** is a normal process; it is affected by the biological traits of an organism as well as physical and biological conditions of the world around them. In the ebb of flow of life on Earth, extinction irrevocably denies the continuance of some species even as it creates new opportunities for those species left behind.

Sometimes the cause of an extinction is so vast and so sudden that hundreds, maybe thousands, of species are affected. A rapid change of this nature that wipes out significant numbers of species is called a mass extinction. Mass extinctions occur rapidly by geologic standards, killing off more than 25 percent of all species in a million years or less.

The subject of mass extinctions often brings to mind the demise of the dinosaurs and visions of Earth being pummeled by a gigantic asteroid. In the history of mass extinctions, however, the geologic events that wiped out the last of the dinosaurs rank only fourth on a list of the five worst mass extinctions. The top three all took place during the Paleozoic Era, long before dinosaurs walked the planet.

CAUSES OF MASS EXTINCTIONS

Mass extinctions change the direction of nearly all life on the planet. Even the most successful lines of organisms can perish when an enormous natural catastrophe makes it impossible for them to recover through the natural course of **adaptation**. Flora and fauna that once dominated **ecosystems** can be wiped out by a mass extinction, leaving ecological niches for other organisms to spread and diversify. So goes the balancing act of nature; when one group of species is devastated, those that survive benefit and continue the evolutionary march of life.

Mass extinctions have many causes and are often the result of multiple, accumulating natural disasters. Even mass extinctions take a long time to unravel Earth's ecosystem—sometimes as long as a million years or more. Mass extinctions are usually caused by widespread changes to both climate and geology. The most common culprits have been:

- *Shifts in Earth's crust.* Movement of tectonic plates can greatly affect the habitat of species. The formation of mountains can change climates and habitats. The joining and separation of landmasses affects climate, ocean depth, near-shore habitats, and the geographic range of species. The Paleozoic Era was an exceptionally active span of tectonic plate movements.
- *Severe climate changes, hot and cold.* If the average temperature of a habitat drops even by only a few degrees, and this change is sustained for months or years, it can severely affect the plants and animals that live in the habitat. Climate changes are often the side effects of other kinds of natural disasters, such as volcanic eruptions, tectonic plate shifts, and meteor or comet strikes. Glaciation on a large scale, such as occurred during the Paleozoic Era, can also lead to worldwide cooling.
- *Massive and continuous volcanic eruptions.* Volcanic action during the Paleozoic Era was often more violent and sustained than anything experienced today. Long periods of volcanic eruption will kill many life-forms living nearby. Volcanoes, however, also can affect habitats worldwide because of the tremendous amounts of smoke and debris they spew into the atmosphere. Airborne debris affects climates by altering both the amount of solar radiation that can penetrate the atmosphere and the amount that is trapped

within the atmosphere. Volcanic gases also may poison the atmosphere by causing acid rain to pour on both land and sea. The Paleozoic Era was capped by one of history's longest and most sustained periods of volcanic activity.

- *Changes in the chemistry of air and water.* The ocean naturally maintains its optimal chemical balance through a complex self-regulatory system called the **global chemostat**. Through this system of natural **feedback** processes, chemical exchanges take place among seawater, the atmosphere, weathering rock, and the metabolic activity of organisms. This equilibrium has been maintained for most of geologic time, but it can be severely tested by natural disasters that may temporarily alter the chemical makeup of the ocean, thereby causing widespread killings of ocean plants and animals. Volcanic eruptions and even asteroid strikes can pulverize minerals in Earth's crust, and these materials can make their way into the oceans. Changes in the acidity or alkalinity of seawater and the presence in the water of toxic substances all can have disastrous effects on sea life, killing off many corals, algae, microorganisms, and plankton. In turn, the destruction of these life-forms eventually devastates communities of animals that depend on those organisms for food and oxygen.

- *Asteroid or comet strikes.* There is a growing body of evidence that Earth has been struck by large asteroids or comets on several occasions, the most famous being the collision that ended the age of the dinosaurs 65 million years ago. A strike of this magnitude would have the explosive power of hundreds of nuclear warheads. Earth's crust would be vaporized at the point of impact. Towering tsunamis, perhaps a mile (1.6 km) or more high, would engulf continental coasts if the event happened to be in mid-ocean. Debris would be launched into the atmosphere, clouding the Sun and possibly polluting the air with toxic gases. This might be followed by globally devastating forest fires that would release thick smoke into the atmosphere. The long-term effects would include such climate changes as a shift in the average global temperature for many hundreds of years. Although asteroid or comet strikes are not currently considered the leading causes of mass extinctions during the Paleozoic Era, they have been implicated in some mass extinctions as a contributing factor, as explained below.

MASS EXTINCTIONS OF THE PALEOZOIC ERA

There were four significant mass extinctions during the Paleozoic Era, three of which rank as the worst in all of geologic history. The Paleozoic Era was a time of great upheaval on Earth. Continents separated and then converged again to form one giant landmass. Seas reached the highest levels seen in the geologic record but also fell back to lows that have rarely occurred again. Even oxygen levels swung from dizzying lows to enormously rich highs, affecting the development of life on land and in the sea. When combined with persistent periods of volcanic eruption, glaciation, and climate shift, it is no wonder that plant and animal life was severely challenged during this era.

End-Cambrian Extinction

The first great extinction of the Paleozoic Era came in the oceans, before the rise of vertebrates and the colonization of the land. The Cambrian was the time of the **trilobites**, bottom-feeding arthropods with a segmented exoskeleton. A trilobite could roll up like a pill bug to defend against attacks by swimming predators such as nautiloids. Trilobites varied widely in size, from a few millimeters to three feet (90 cm) long. They and other creatures represented in the Burgess Shale—a significant deposit of Cambrian fossils in British Columbia, Canada—lived in shallow ocean environments and on reefs. Trilobites evolved during the Early Cambrian Epoch along with early crabs, marine worms, sea pens, and various other mysterious shelled creatures that remain unclassifiable using today's **extant** (existing) phyla. Trilobites were particularly robust, and they

A trilobite fossil

grew in diversity and oceanic range until well into the Permian Period.

The end of the Cambrian Period saw violent shifts in Earth's tectonic plates and widespread volcanic eruptions. These geologic effects caused several drops in the level of the sea. Over many hundreds of years, this transformed the shallow-water habitats occupied by some of the most plentiful and wondrous Cambrian creatures. Some near-shore environments dried under the Sun as ocean waters retreated time and time again. While many phyla of animals adapted successfully to the changing conditions, nearly half (42 percent) could not and became extinct. Among those that became extinct were the oldest species of trilobites, some brachiopods, early reef-building organisms, and some species of early eel-like vertebrates known as conodonts. The end-Cambrian mass extinction brought the end of a way of life that had reigned supreme in the oceans for many millions of years. Although the trilobites continued to prosper in various forms, their reign as one of the most successful ocean creatures was gradually diminished by the development of other more mobile and diverse life-forms.

Ordovician–Silurian Extinction

With the coming of the Ordovician Period, the ocean's ecosystems were vastly reshaped from what they had been during the Cambrian Period. By the start of the Ordovician Period, sea levels were substantially higher over those of the Early Cambrian. The oceans were still warm, but they were deeper and more varied in the kinds of habitats available than they had been during the Cambrian Period. In addition to near-shore environments, oceans developed tiers of habitable domains at various depths, thereby encouraging the evolution of a diverse community of new creatures. Among these were corals; cephalopods (mollusks, including the first species of nautiluses); the stalked, bottom-feeding crinoids; the mosslike and branchlike colonial-living bryozoans; gastropods (single-shelled creatures such as snails); and bivalves (two-shelled creatures such as clams). The Ordovician was also a time of gradually increasing diversity of the first vertebrates, including conodonts and the first fishes, known as jawless fishes.

The appearance of nautiloids and jawless fishes marked an escalating race of predatory, free-swimming creatures. The nautiloids, especially the coiled species, were active hunters. They fed on trilobites, further decimating the lines of surviving trilobites with roots in the Cambrian era.

The end of the Ordovician Period witnessed the second most devastating mass extinction on record, second only to the extinction that ended the Paleozoic Era. The cause of the Ordovician-Silurian extinction event was probably global cooling, most likely precipitated by major glaciation on the southern part of the Gondwana supercontinent. This cooled the shallowest parts of the sea, killing off many species in tropical ocean regions. One-third of the bryozoans and brachiopods were killed off. Conodonts and trilobites took additional hits. Crinoids and other reef community invertebrates were greatly reduced, and many families of nautiloids disappeared. Across the planet, more than 100 families of marine invertebrates—about 85 percent of all marine animal species—perished at that time. Supporting the theory that the Ordovician-Silurian extinction was caused by global cooling is the fact that the survivors of this devastation were either from deeper, colder waters, or from colder climates where the species had already become well adapted to cooler temperatures.

Late Devonian Extinction

Following the extensive extinction at the end of the Ordovician, moving continents once again played a role in determining the direction that life was about to take. The proximity of the poles to landmasses or ocean can result in climate changes. If the poles are located in open ocean, they will be warmer than if they are located on landmasses. During the early stages of the Silurian Period, the supercontinent Gondwana drifted away from the South Pole, leading to warmer oceans worldwide. During this time, life rebounded; this rebound led to the proliferation of jawless fishes and cephalopod relatives of the nautiloids known as ammonites or ammonoids. The first jawed fishes also appeared but were not yet as dominant as predators as they would become later. Ammonoids were likely the most important ocean predators of the time, cruising the open tropical oceans in large groups and grabbing prey with their tentacles.

The Silurian Period remained warm and hospitable to tropical life, but by the Early to Middle Devonian Epoch, the continent of Gondwana had slipped back over the South Pole, causing another intense period of glaciation in the Southern Hemisphere. As in the Ordovician-Silurian extinction, the effect of the cooling was again severe for many invertebrates. The circulation of cold waters across the oceans also may have dredged up nonoxygenated waters to the surface. This mass extinction took its toll during a five-million-year span of the Late Devonian Epoch, eventually killing off many ocean species in tropical waters. As many as 70 percent of the world's marine invertebrates were wiped out. Among them were many species of brachiopods, ammonoids, trilobites, and reef community fauna. Among vertebrates, many of the developing species of Devonian fish were decimated, particularly the armored jawless fishes but also some of the placoderms, the first jawed fishes.

By the end of the Devonian, the oceans were receding, as northern landmasses moved closer together. With the retreat of glaciers in Gondwana, the oceans once again warmed up, setting the stage for the colonization of land by plant and animal life.

Permian–Triassic Extinction

The worst mass extinction of all time occurred 251 million years ago, at the end of the Permian Period. Fossil evidence shows that life on Earth nearly came to an abrupt halt at that time. As many as 95 percent of all ocean species were erased. Gone from the seas were most crinoids, brachiopods, reef-building bryozoans, nautiloids, and ammonoids. Nearly every marine invertebrate group suffered huge losses; most groups never regained the diversity that they once had. Land animals were hit nearly as hard. By the end of the Permian Period, 75 percent of all terrestrial vertebrate taxa had been wiped out. Among them were six families of archaic vertebrates representing early amphibians, reptiles, and synapsids, including several families of formidable saurian predators.

Despite the obvious severity of this mass extinction, its cause and effects have been a matter of debate for as long as the Permian Period has been recognized as a distinct geologic stratum, or layer within geologic fossil history. The geologist responsible for naming the Permian stratum was Scotsman Roderick Impey Murchison (1792–1871). Murchison, a wealthy man and a former soldier, took up geologic exploration at the urging of his friend, paleontologist William Buckland (1784–1856). Buckland was the scientist responsible for writing the first scientific description of a dinosaur. Early in his geologic career, Murchison made extensive surveys of strata in Scotland and Europe and contributed one of the first notable studies of fossil fish. His enthusiastic work brought him to the attention of other well-known naturalists of the time, including Adam Sedgwick (1785–1873), professor of geology at Cambridge University. Working with Sedgwick, the two named the Devonian geologic stratum in 1839. That stratum is also known as the Old Red Sandstone, a thick, reddish stratigraphic zone rich with marine fossils. The Old Red Sandstone can be traced through regions of Wales, Scotland, England, and Northern Ireland.

Murchison had a voracious appetite for exploration and kept meticulous records about fossils that he came upon in his fieldwork. Soon after his success in the British Isles, the Scotsman set off to explore Russia. While studying formations in eastern Russia, Murchison recognized a fossil-bearing layer with marked differences over those previously discovered. This layer was positioned over the deposits of the Carboniferous Period, a widely known stratigraphic layer also found in Europe. The Russian formation contained fossils distinctly different from those Murchison had seen before. In 1841, the Scotsman named this formation—which he described as a "vast series of beds of marls, schists, limestones, sandstones, and conglomerates"—the Permian, after the city of Perm in Russia's Ural Mountains.

What made Murchison's newly christened Permian Period a source of controversy was that its strata contained a rich trove of fossil organisms that suddenly disappeared from overlying sediments in the wink of a moment in geologic time. Murchison interpreted this evidence as the telltale sign of a catastrophic extinction of life—a truly radical and unpopular suggestion in mid-nineteenth-century Europe. Murchison made this extraordinary claim with little more corroboration than his single stratum of previously undiscovered **sedimentary rock** and a hunch. The very concept of mass extinction was itself viewed as heretical and antireligious, an affront to God's ability to create and sustain life. According to paleontologist Michael Benton (b. 1956) of the University of Bristol, Murchison's discovery was so startling that even some of the most respected naturalists of 1841, including Charles Darwin (1809–1882) and Robert Lyell (1797–1875), were compelled to explain away the apparent disappearance of Permian fossil species as a mere gap in the fossil record rather than as a mass extinction. In time, with the discovery of similar gaps in Permian deposits at other geologic locations, paleontologists accepted the fact that the end of the Paleozoic Era marked a truly horrendous loss of species, the likes of which has never evolved again.

Causes and Timing of the Permian-Triassic Extinction

Even after having established the severity of the Permian-Triassic extinction, geologists and paleontologists have puzzled for many years over the cause of the catastrophe. Unlike other extinction events for which causes have been more clearly attributed, such as the killer asteroid that ended the reign of the dinosaurs 65 million years ago, the Permian-Triassic extinction and the events leading up to it are more geologically complicated. Physical evidence from the Late Paleozoic Era is clouded by a swarm of many interrelated factors that may have affected the course of life. A bevy of potential culprits have been identified, including continental shifts, changes in sea level, global cooling due to glaciation, global warming, changes in ocean chemistry, volcanic eruptions, and speculation that at the end of the Permian Period, the planet may have been struck by an asteroid.

The list of killer suspects seems almost endless in this case. Consider the following mixed bag of natural disasters. Climates changed dramatically during the Middle Permian. Warm, tropical ocean currents that once flowed between equatorial landmasses became restricted to the perimeter of the supercontinent as landmasses moved together and tropical areas became landlocked. This restricted habitats and essentially trapped indigenous species. The lower reaches of Pangaea were positioned over the South Pole. This caused glaciers to form as they had in the Ordovician and Devonian Periods. Both of these cooling events coincided with the forming of the supercontinent Pangaea, a landmass so large that it stretched from the North Pole to the South Pole. A massive ice sheet measuring 0.6 miles (1 km) thick in places appeared in Siberia, marking the first time in Earth's history that significant ice belts appeared at the same time in both the Northern and Southern Hemispheres. Global cooling probably led to sea level drops, to extended droughts that formed desert zones on Pangaea, and to a global shift to distinct climate zones to which some species could not adequately adapt. This entire sequence was brought to an end with an extended period of volcanic activity in the Northern Hemisphere.

The length of the Permian mass extinction was also a matter of debate for many years. Some scientists believed that the extinction took place gradually, over many millions of years, and that it probably was spurred by an escalating sequence of different but interconnected causes. One scenario suggested that there were two extinction events: a smaller one that followed Middle Permian glaciation and climate shifts, and a larger one at the end of the Permian that was triggered by a worldwide geologic cataclysm of some type. This uncertainty has led to arguments about the timing of the end of the extinction, with estimates ranging from 225 million to 250 million years ago—a range of 25 million years.

The major challenges for scientists trying to resolve the issues related to the causes and timing of the Permian-Triassic extinction were, first, to establish the reasons for the extinction and, second, to quantify the rate at which so many species perished.

How Most Life Can Perish

The unraveling of the Permian-Triassic extinction mystery did not come all of a sudden, with a single, startling new discovery. The cause became evident step by step, through research conducted by a number of scientific teams working on several fronts.

Several well-studied stratigraphic layers around the world document the fossil record of the Late Permian Epoch. These include sites in Antarctica, Austria, southern China, Greenland, Iran, Italy, Japan, Pakistan, and South Africa. Of these sites, a fossil locality in southern China—a site known as the Meishan section after a nearby town—has become a key to unraveling some of the biggest questions about the Permian-Triassic catastrophe. This site was first studied by Chinese scientists in the 1970s and 1980s. It became evident to those working there that the Meishan formation was startlingly complete for a stratigraphic layer. During the past twenty years, research spearheaded by Jin Yugan (b. 1937) of the Nanjing Institute of Geology and Paleontology has made the Meishan formation the world's best indicator of what truly happened at the end of the Permian Period. During the 1990s, as China began to open its doors more widely to foreign scientists, Jin and other Chinese scientists invited several geologists and paleontologists from outside the country to take a closer look at the Meishan. The result of this international cooperation was that the jigsaw puzzle of the Permian-Triassic extinction finally began to take shape. The overall picture looks something like what follows.

Precise dating of the extinction. In 1998, a team consisting of British, Chinese, and American scientists used radiometric dating to establish an accurate timing for the Permian-Triassic extinction. The extinction event was dated to about 251 million years ago.

Extent of the mass extinction. In 2000, Jin Yugan and his American colleague Douglas H. Erwin (b. 1958) of the National Museum of Natural History of the Smithsonian Institution published the results of a comprehensive census of species and extinctions from the Meishan formation. This census revealed that 94 percent of marine species found at Meishan were wiped out. The extinction began with the elimination of 116 marine species and continued with the disappearance of 45 more species in the following 500,000 years. This marks a rapid and disastrous depletion of marine organisms.

Evidence for a cause. The stratigraphic layer that represents the mass extinction is topped by three layers that are virtually devoid of life. Furthermore, the composition of each layer tells a story of its own. Immediately above the extinction layer is a thin layer of clay containing very few fossils. The clay of this layer is infused with iron-rich particles and tiny shards of quartz. These indicate that the ocean was pelted with ash from a massive volcanic eruption. The next sedimentary layer up contains a few fossils of clams, brachiopods, and cephalopods. These suggest that a slow recovery was under way. On top of that is another layer, this time of limestone. Although fossils are still relatively sparse in this layer, the appearance of new species occurs for the first time in the fossil record since the end of the Permian-Triassic mass extinction.

The timing of this stratigraphic evidence coincides with a record of massive volcanic activity in Russia known as the Siberian Traps. These eruptions were extensive, lasted for nearly a million years, and coincided with the Permian-Triassic mass extinction. The Siberian Traps were the most catastrophic episode of sustained volcanic eruption of the past 542 million years. The lava discharge equaled more than 360,000 cubic miles (1.5 million cubic km) and now covers an area of 130,100 square miles (337,000 square km) of Siberia. If one could spread this amount of lava evenly over the whole Earth, it would form a layer 10 feet (3 m) thick.

There have also been claims that the Permian-Triassic extinction was triggered by the impact of a large asteroid with the Earth—the kind of colossal accident that would have blackened the sky, poisoned the oceans, and left the planet starving for sunlight for many years. A similar scenario has been widely accepted as the final blow in the extinction of the dinosaurs. The case for the Permian-Triassic impact has been championed by Luann Becker (b. 1960) and colleagues at the University of California, Santa Barbara, and a team of NASA scientists. Becker's original claims were impressive; they were based on chemical analysis of sediments from the same Meishan fossil locality in China that was used to determine the timing of the extinction. Unfortunately, attempts by other scientists to reproduce

Becker's test results have so far been unsuccessful. As of this writing, Becker's impact theory for the Permian-Triassic extinction does not hold up to scrutiny as well as the volcanic-eruption hypothesis.

The effects of massive volcanic activity. Volcanism occurring at the extreme levels of the Siberian Traps would have released massive amounts of CO_2 and other chemicals into the atmosphere. A thick barrier of smoky clouds may have blocked sunlight from reaching Earth's surface and so played havoc with plant life and photosynthesis on land and sea. As plants and animals died, more CO_2 would have been released. The greenhouse effect could have made the climate and oceans warmer, perhaps by as much as 11°F (6°C)—a relatively enormous shift that would have led to catastrophic habitat changes and a disruption of the natural chemical feedback system of the global chemostat. According to paleontologist Michael Benton, this rise in temperature would have warmed the oceans enough to cause them to release a vast store of methane that had been safely stored away in the cold deep at the bottom of the sea. Normally, when methane surges, it uses oxygen in the water or air to form carbon dioxide. But what happens when there is more methane than even the vast stores of oceanic oxygen can counteract? The Permian "methane burp," as Benton calls it, would have been so large as to overwhelm Earth's normal feedback systems, releasing vast stores of carbon dioxide into the air.

Worldwide oxygen levels would have plummeted, the oceans would have begun to suffer from **anoxia**—a lack of oxygen—and life would have begun to die. A runaway greenhouse effect would have taken over, killing off plankton in the oceans and triggering a life-shattering reign of death that decimated marine life. Terrestrial animals also would be affected by a global warming. Plants would die, as would those animals that depended on plants for food and those animals that ate the plant eaters.

The animals that perished in the Permian oceans were largely immobile and sedentary, unable to escape the oxygen deprivation of their habitat. Of the 5 percent of ocean creatures that survived, including fishes, mollusks, and arthropods, each species was more mobile and was equipped with a more robust gill system for extracting what little oxygen was left in the water.

MASS EXTINCTIONS OF THE PALEOZOIC ERA

Extinction Event	Time (Millions of Years Ago)	Extent	Cause	Most Dramatic Casualties
End-Cambrian extinction	485	About 42% of marine animal species perished.	Tectonic plate shifts, volcanic eruptions, drop in sea level	Brachiopods, conodonts, and trilobites
Ordovician-Silurian extinction	440	About 85% of marine animal species perished.	Glaciation and lower sea levels	Trilobites, echinoderms, and nautiloids
Late-Devonian extinction	374	About 70% of marine animal species perished.	Glaciation and global cooling, partly resulting from tectonic plate movements	Ammonoids, trilobites, gastropods, reef community fauna, armored jawless fish, and placoderms
Permian-Triassic extinction	251	About 95% of marine animal species and 75% of terrestrial animal species perished.	Extensive volcanic activity, lower sea levels, oceanic methane belches causing anoxia in the oceans and massive release of CO_2	95% of all ocean species; 75% of land vertebrates

EXTINCTION AND RECOVERY: AN ECOLOGICAL SHAKEDOWN

The Paleozoic Era was marked by four mass extinctions, two of which were the most devastating of all time. In the worst case, 251 million years ago, all life came to within a whisper of being annihilated. According to Michael Benton, the Permian-Triassic extinction was so severe that it took nearly 100 million years for global biodiversity to return to preextinction levels—a span that is a third as long as the entire Paleozoic Era.

But news of mass extinction was not bad for all species. The Paleozoic mass extinctions opened up niches in the ecosystem for other organisms to fill. After each natural catastrophe, surviving families of invertebrates and vertebrates were able to move into newly forming or vacated domains. By the Middle Paleozoic, the vertebrates in particular became increasingly diverse and abundant; they supplanted invertebrates that had once ruled the world's habitats.

SUMMARY

This chapter reviewed mass extinctions of the Paleozoic Era, their causes, and their effect on the direction of life.

1. Mass extinctions occur rapidly by geologic standards; they kill off more than 25 percent of all species in a million years or less.
2. Mass extinctions are usually caused by widespread changes to both climate and geology.
3. Common causes behind mass extinctions include shifts in the Earth's crust, severe climate swings, massive and continuous volcanic eruptions, changes to the chemistry of air or water, and strikes by asteroids or comets.
4. There were four significant mass extinctions during the Paleozoic Era; two of them rank as the worst extinctions in all of geologic history.
5. The mass extinctions of the Paleozoic Era were the end-Cambrian extinction, the Ordovician-Silurian extinction, the Late Devonian extinction, and the Permian-Triassic extinction.
6. The worst mass extinction of all time was the Permian-Triassic extinction, which occurred 251 million years ago. It wiped out 95 percent of marine species and 75 percent of land vertebrate taxa.
7. The Permian-Triassic extinction occurred rapidly, during a span of 500,000 years.
8. The Permian-Triassic extinction was triggered by massive prolonged volcanic activity in Siberia, a runaway greenhouse

effect, and the plummeting of worldwide oxygen levels due to disruption of Earth's natural chemostat.

9. Recovery of species from the Permian-Triassic extinction was slow; it required about 100 million years for global biodiversity to return to preextinction levels.

10. Mass extinctions open up niches in the ecosystem for other organisms to fill.

SECTION TWO:
THE FIRST VERTEBRATES

3

VERTEBRATE TRAITS

Every individual fossil is a rare and revealing artifact. It reveals secrets about the form, structure, and perhaps even the lifestyle of a long extinct organism. That, however, is not the whole story. An individual fossil is also part of a long history of evolutionary life. A fossil is like a single domino in a long series of dominoes. Each one is affected by the one that came just before it. Our knowledge of past life greatly expands when we can connect individual fossils with other, similar kinds of fossils and the habitats in which they once lived.

The work of a paleontologist does not take place entirely in the field, with rock hammer in hand. Although many thousands of scientists have collected vast numbers of fossils from sites all across Earth, the job of studying and comparing these artifacts and pulling together the information they impart is even more daunting than the initial collection. Without such analysis, individual fossils remain as single, isolated dominoes, detached from the mainstream of life's evolutionary story.

Paleontologist J. John Sepkoski Jr. (1948–1999) was a leading figure in the field of paleobiology during the past 30 years. He had a passion for data analysis. Sepkoski attacked the fossil record not with a pick and shovel, but with a computer and a genius for recognizing patterns among vast stores of information about fossil specimens. By assimilating data from many fossil discoveries, he was able to fill gaps in the rich history of life and shape an increasingly cohesive picture of the evolution of organisms.

Sepkoski conducted exhaustive and comprehensive studies of the fossil record. He pioneered the use of statistical analysis and computer modeling to extrapolate data about the diversification of life over the millennia. In the early 1980s, he began to release findings that documented the ups and downs of life on Earth over 600 million years. Sepkoski's data were applied, by himself and others, to a wide range of paleontological disciplines, including evolutionary theory, studies of paleohabitats, animal diversification, and mass extinctions. So influential was Sepkoski's work that during the 1980s and 1990s, many of his colleagues regularly included his data and figures in their own studies.

Some of Sepkoski's greatest work was focused on the animal life of the Paleozoic. Through his data, he originated the idea that the planet has been dominated by three important and distinct faunas, which he called the Cambrian, the Paleozoic, and the Modern.

The Cambrian fauna lived at the beginning of the Paleozoic Era and included the archaic invertebrates that formed the roots of most subsequent animal species. Typical Cambrian fauna included trilobites, early mollusks, and other arthropods.

The Paleozoic fauna took over in the Ordovician Period, after the extinction of many Cambrian species. The Paleozoic fauna were marked by the adaptive radiation and diversification of many successful and enduring marine invertebrates. Moving into a broader range of ocean habitats, the Paleozoic fauna were at home in coastal shallows as well as in tiered and open ocean environments. Bottom-feeding brachiopods, crinoids, and bryozoans were complemented by predatory nautiloids and other early cephalopods that swam freely. Many species of Paleozoic fauna came and went, but together they dominated the marine fauna of the planet until the great Permian-Triassic extinction.

The Paleozoic fauna were followed, in the Mesozoic and Cenozoic Eras, by what Sepkoski called the Modern fauna—the kinds of animals that still exist in the oceans and on land. Among the Modern fauna are the vertebrates. Although the vertebrates did not begin to dominate life on Earth until the early Mesozoic Era, their roots are found in the Paleozoic. This chapter introduces the **anatomy** of the vertebrates, their origins, and their first successful adaptive radiation in the sea as fishes.

THE CHORDATES

Vertebrates are members of the phylum Chordata, a group of organisms with roots in the Early Cambrian Epoch. At some time in their life, all chordates have an internal, rodlike supporting structure known as a **notochord**, a nerve cord running on top of the notochord, and gill slits or lungs for breathing.

Phylum **Chordata** is made up of three subphyla: the **Urochordata**, **Cephalochordata**, and **Vertebrata**. Both the Urochordata and Cephalochordata are chordates that lack skulls.

Typical living urochordates include sea squirts, tunicates, and ascidians, all of which have larvae that are free-swimming and adults that are **benthic**—seafloor dwelling and stationary. The adults measure from .04 to 4.9 inches (1 to 120 mm) long; they have a bulbous, plantlike appearance and lack most affinities with the other chordates. These baglike animals use muscles to contract and expand their bodies; they suck in seawater to trap nutrients in the form of phytoplankton. As unchordatelike as adult urochordates seem, their larval, tadpolelike young have typical chordate features, including a notochord, a **dorsal** hollow nerve cord, and gill slits. All urochordates are marine creatures; they make up 90 percent of the chordates without backbones. There are about 1,250 living varieties of urochordates.

The cephalochordates measure from 2 to 6 inches (5 to 15 cm) in length. They are small filter feeders and live on sandy, shallow seafloors. The three defining traits of chordates—a stiff notochord, a dorsal nerve cord, and gills slits—are retained by cephalochordates even in adulthood. One familiar group of cephalochordates are the lancelets. They feed by darting into the sand and burying their bodies with only the head end exposed. Tiny tentacles on the head grab nutrient particles from seawater. Only 23 species of living cephalochordates are known, making them the least populous members of phylum Chordata. Although cephalochordates lack a backbone, comparison of their **gene** sequences to that of vertebrates confirms

A sea squirt

A branchiostoma

that lancelets and their kind are the closest invertebrate relatives to animals with backbones.

Vertebrates make up the largest subphylum of chordates. There are more than 48,000 living species of snakes, fish, monkeys, rodents, and other familiar backboned animals, compared to only about 1,275 living species of invertebrate chordates. Even so, vertebrates are vastly outnumbered by other invertebrate creatures in the world and make up only about 5 percent of all known living species of animals on land and sea. Despite being outnumbered, the relatively large size, mobility, and intelligence of vertebrates allows them to dominate any ecological niche in which they naturally occur. So, even though invertebrate fossils are readily more obtainable and outnumber vertebrate fossils by a large percentage, many paleontologists are irresistibly drawn to ponder the history of vertebrates because these organisms represent the roots of humans and the other backboned creatures with which we most commonly interact in the world.

ANATOMY OF THE VERTEBRATES

Vertebrates include fishes, amphibians, reptiles, mammals, and birds. As a group of related organisms, vertebrates share several anatomical

Bilateral Symmetry

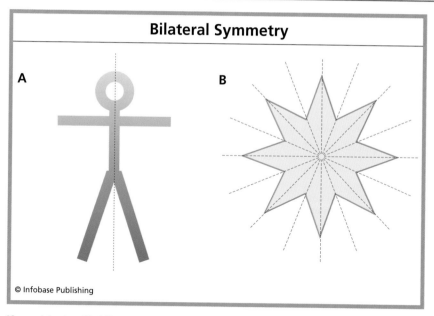

A   B

© Infobase Publishing

If an object with bilateral symmetry were divided in half or into equal sections, each half or section would be identical to the other half or sections.

features, although the specific nature of these characteristics will vary widely from **taxon** to taxon. These anatomical features include:

- *Bilateral symmetry.* A fundamental feature of vertebrates is a body plan that is bilaterally symmetrical: One side of the body is a mirror image of the other. Some invertebrates share this same kind of symmetry in their body plan, most notably **annelid** worms and arthropods, including insects, crabs, spiders, and others. In vertebrates, **bilateral symmetry** results in pairs of features such as two eyes, two ears, and two pairs of limbs.
- *Backbone.* In vertebrates, the notochord takes the form of a series of bony vertebrae that run lengthwise down the midline of the back of the body, forming the vertebral, or spinal, column, which is also known as the backbone or spine.
- *Internal skeleton.* Along with the spinal column, vertebrates have an internal, axially oriented skeleton that is made of either bone or **cartilage**. In most vertebrates, the skeleton is

made of bone. An **axial** skeleton is one in which the body develops lengthwise along an axis. In vertebrates, the spinal column forms the axis, with a skull at the **anterior**, or head, end and usually with ribs attached to the vertebrae to form the outline of the body cavity, or trunk. An internal skeleton is also known as an **endoskeleton**.

- *Appendicular skeleton.* In addition to the axial skeleton, most vertebrates have paired legs or fins for locomotion. These **appendicular** limb elements are attached to the body by bony girdles and muscles.
- *Skull.* Sense organs and the brain form the nerve center of a vertebrate; they are usually housed in a protective skull at the anterior end of the body.
- *Segmented muscles.* The muscles of the vertebrate trunk are segmented and fibrous; they provide a wide range of flex and locomotion.
- *Pharynx.* In most vertebrates, the **pharynx** is an inconspicuous connection between the mouth and the esophagus or throat—a mere passage through which air, water, or food can pass. From an evolutionary standpoint, however, the pharynx is important because it is the location of gill pouches in early vertebrates—a region that represents the root design of respiration in all vertebrates.
- *Gills or lungs.* Vertebrates have either gills to extract oxygen from water or lungs to extract oxygen from air.
- *Spinal nerve chord and circulatory and digestive systems.* Vertebrates have the spinal cord positioned above the notochord or spinal column. The circulatory and respiratory systems are located on the other side of the spinal column, in the trunk of the body.

Knowing these anatomical characteristics allows one to understand the basic design of all vertebrates. Familiarity with the anatomy of one kind of vertebrate provides insight into the workings of all vertebrates because the skeletons, organs, and even the behavior of different vertebrate taxa are similar in many ways. From this realization comes the principle of homology. **Homologies** are traits that different species of organisms have inherited from a common ancestor. Homologies are the basis for our knowledge of how organisms are related.

Understanding the anatomical characteristics and homologies that unite all vertebrates provides greater insight into the nature of extinct members of the subphylum Vertebrata. This knowledge allows a paleontologist to surmise about the skeleton of an extinct animal even if major portions of that skeleton are missing. Understanding living vertebrates provides basic information about the **physiology** of extinct taxa and how they may have behaved.

Bones and Hard Tissues

One characteristic that distinguishes vertebrates from animals without backbones (invertebrates) is the presence of **cellular bone**, a form of bone that lives and grows as tissue. Cellular bone contains channels for blood vessels and is made of **apatite**, or calcium phosphate. In contrast, the skeletal structures of most invertebrates are made mostly of calcium compounds and appear visibly different when viewed under a microscope. Cellular bone is not found in any invertebrate. Cellular bone is associated with the vertebrate endoskeleton and may be found in any skeletal part of the body, not only the spinal column.

As states above, one of the ingredients of vertebrate bones is the mineral apatite, or calcium phosphate. Apatite is one of the building blocks of cellular bone and is also found in teeth, in the form of **dentine** and **enamel**. The **dermal** armor or scales of some vertebrates are sometimes made of the same material as teeth. The armor plating of early vertebrates had more in common with teeth than with the cellular bone that would evolve later.

CLUES TO THE FIRST VERTEBRATES

Paleontologists in search of the earliest vertebrates look for many of the anatomical features associated with backboned animals.

(continues on page 64)

THINK ABOUT IT

Which End Is Up? Labeling Directions Within the Vertebrate Body Plan

The bilaterally symmetrical body plan of vertebrates provides paleontologists and zoologists with an opportunity to share common terms and effectively communicate with one another as they describe the anatomy direction and overall structure of such animals. These terms allow precision in the description of the location of an organ, a bone, or even just a part of an organ or bone.

In most animals, the head and tail ends also indicate the direction in which the animal moves. The terms *anterior* (or **cranial**) and **posterior** (or *caudal*) are normally used to describe the head and tail ends respectively. The upper and lower surfaces of an animal—the back and belly—are described as the **dorsal** (back) and **ventral** (underside) surfaces. The terms *cranial* and *caudal* are also used to indicate the proximity of a part to either the head or tail, as in a "caudal" vertebra, which would be located in the tail region of the spine.

Humans, by standing upright, require a slightly modified version of these terms because humans' cranial end—the head—is not the end that represents the direction in which humans move. Instead, the term *superior* (or cranial) has been adapted to describe the upright head end of a human and the term *inferior* (or caudal) is used to describe the lower, or foot end. In humans, the terms *anterior* and *ventral* are synonymous, as are the terms *posterior* and *dorsal*.

Two additional, though less precise, directional terms are used to better describe the positional relationship that a given part of the anatomy has to the whole body. The term **proximal** describes a part that is closer to the center of the body of the animal; the term **distal** describes a part that is positioned toward the outside of the body. A bone in the leg, for example, has a proximal end and a distal end. These terms are widely

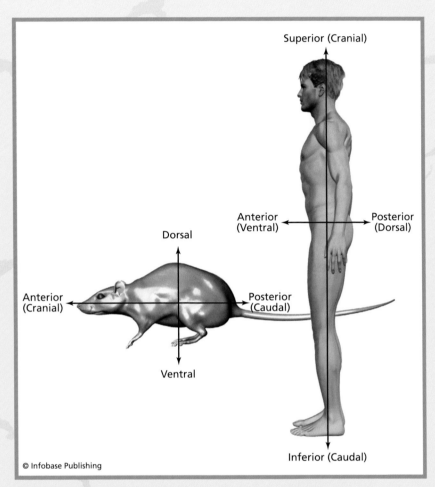

Superior (Cranial)

Anterior
(Ventral)

Posterior
(Dorsal)

Dorsal

Anterior
(Cranial)

Posterior
(Caudal)

Ventral

Inferior (Caudal)

© Infobase Publishing

Positional terms used to describe vertebrate anatomy

used by paleontologists, as they try to piece together the picture of an entire creature, to describe the positions of the bones and bone fragments that they have found.

(continued from page 61)

The presence of a skull and bony skeleton in a fossil are obvious giveaways, but fossils of the earliest vertebrates are both notoriously incomplete and so **basal** that they do not exhibit any obvious anatomical structures. Some specimens may consist of body impressions left in the stone rather than actual fossilized hard body parts. Such impressions can show outlines of organs and soft tissues that perhaps reveal signs of vertebrate affinities such as gills, eyes, and other soft parts.

One of the most reliable indicators of a vertebrate animal is the presence of apatite in its hard body parts. Given that some of the earliest fossil evidence of early animals consists only of scales, possible teeth, and fragmentary hard tissues, the presence of apatite in these fossils becomes a kind of litmus test for separating early vertebrates from invertebrates. The evolution of the vertebrates began in the oceans of the Early Cambrian Epoch.

SUMMARY

This chapter introduced the anatomy of the vertebrates, their origins, and their first successful adaptive radiation in the sea as fishes.

1. Earth has been dominated by three important and distinct faunas: the Cambrian marine invertebrates, the Paleozoic marine invertebrates, and the Modern marine and terrestrial vertebrates.
2. The Modern fauna, which appeared following the end of the Paleozoic Era, are dominated by vertebrates with roots in the Paleozoic.
3. Vertebrates are members of the phylum Chordata, a group of organisms that share an internal, rodlike supporting structure known as a notochord; a nerve cord that runs on top of the notochord; and gill slits or lungs for breathing.
4. Vertebrates are animals with backbones; they make up the largest subphylum of chordates. There are more than 48,000

living species of backboned animals compared to only about 1,275 species of invertebrate chordates.

5. Distinguishing characteristics of vertebrates include bilateral symmetry, a backbone, an internal skeleton, two pairs of appendicular limb elements, a skull, segmented muscles, a pharynx, gills or lungs, a spinal nerve chord, a circulatory system, and a digestive system.

6. Homologies are traits that different species of organisms have inherited from a common ancestor.

7. One characteristic that distinguishes vertebrates from animals without backbones is the presence of cellular bone.

4

VERTEBRATE ORIGINS

To accept J. John Sepkoski's calculations regarding the diversification of marine taxa over time is to accept that vertebrates are truly evolutionary latecomers—sophisticated creatures that crashed the party of invertebrates that had reigned for 291 million years of the Paleozoic. Sepkoski showed that the Paleozoic was dominated by a great diversification of animals without backbones and that vertebrates were waiting in the background for their opportunity to rise.

Until recently, the best fossil evidence suggested that the first vertebrates appeared during the Late Cambrian and Early Ordovician Epochs. The rise of fishes in the Late Ordovician, about 450 million years ago, was considered the first significant radiation of animals with backbones. Recent discoveries, however, have now pushed the appearance of the first known vertebrates back to the Early Cambrian, about 525 million years ago, near the explosion of life at the dawn of the Paleozoic. The earliest of these backboned animals was discovered in 1999. Ironically, its remains may have been unintentionally overlooked for many years by paleontologists who scoured the same rock formations in China in search of specimens of larger, more abundant invertebrate remains. It is now clearly evident that ancestral fishes lived in the watery shadows of an invertebrate world, cowering in the presence of crabs, giant sea scorpions, hungry ammonoids, and a seafloor crawling with trilobites.

THE FIRST CHORDATES

For many years, the earliest known chordates were members of the subphylum Cephalochordata that lacked backbones and were superficially related to the eel-like living cephalochordates. Evidence for the existence of these creatures was far less common than fossils of invertebrates from the time, but scientists hailed specimens of these chordates from the Early Cambrian Chengjiang formation of southern China and the Middle Cambrian Burgess Shale deposits of western Canada as the earliest traces of animals within the same phylum as animals with backbones. These ribbonlike creatures swam the shallow Cambrian seas and included such species as *Haikouella* and *Yunnanozoon* from China and *Pikaia* from the Burgess Shale of western Canada.

The remarkable preservation of these creatures in finely grained mudstone shows soft tissues and the unmistakable traits of chordate anatomy: an elongate body plan with an axial notochord and band-like muscles. Conspicuously absent from these chordates was a true backbone and any evidence of cellular bone; this suggests that their skeletons were cartilaginous. Measuring only one to two inches (28 to 50 mm) long, these sliverlike animals were free swimmers that wriggled along in the water powered by the bands of muscles encircling their bodies. They fed by scooping food into their mouths as they swam. In a world dominated by armor-plated arthropods and vicious predators with a startling array of claws and jaws, the early chordates were remarkable because of their conspicuous lack of protection. How they managed to survive is unknown, but one can surmise that they were able-enough swimmers to elude often the clench of attacking predators.

Pikaia was the first of these slivery creatures to be recognized as a chordate. This little creature was first misidentified as an extinct segmented worm in 1911 by Charles Walcott (1850–1927), the discoverer of the Burgess Shale fossil beds in which it was found. Additional specimens of this two-inch (51 mm) "worm" popped up from the Burgess Shale over the years, sometimes revealing more detail than that which Walcott had at his disposal. Over time, *Pikaia* was provisionally thought to be an early chordate, but it was not until 1979, when then–graduate student Simon Conway Morris (b. 1951) was given the task of classifying the Burgess Shale worms, that *Pikaia's* true status as a chordate was substantiated. By 1991, similar fossil chordates were also being discovered in the Chengjiang formation in China. These discoveries in China pushed the earliest known species of chordates back to the Early Cambrian Epoch, about 525 million years ago.

The story of Early Cambrian chordates does not end with the ribbonlike cephalochordates. Recent discoveries have revealed that cephalochordates were not the only members of the chordate clan to have occupied the Early Cambrian seas. The evolutionary position of these extinct cephalochordates that once were considered ancestral to the vertebrates is now in question due to the discovery of vertebrate creatures that lived among them.

VERTEBRATE BEGINNINGS

The transition to the Modern fauna of vertebrates was well underway during the Middle Paleozoic with the evolution of the first marine animals with backbones. With some exceptions mentioned in this chapter, the earliest vertebrates are known only from scant fossil records of the Cambrian and Ordovician Periods found in western Scotland, North America, South Africa, Australia, and Bolivia, and consist largely of dermal armor, feeding apparatus, and bony plates. These creatures are classified as the earliest **Agnatha** ("no jaw") or jawless fishes, a collection of all known early marine vertebrates that predate the development of bony jaws. The evolutionary relationships among the Agnatha are sketchy and little known due to the scarcity of their fossils. What is plain is that fishes without jaws developed before fishes with jaws, and paleontologists continue to work on finding evolutionary links between them using available fossil evidence.

The best known specimens of the extinct fishes from the Cambrian Period are from the groups Myllokunmingiida and Conodonta. Both provide a glimpse at the earliest form of ancestral vertebrate creatures.

The Myllokunmingiida

In 1999, paleontologist Degan Shu and his colleagues at the China University of Geosciences in Beijing announced the spectacular discovery of the earliest known vertebrate, the jawless fish *Myllokunmingia*. Found among fossils of splendidly preserved invertebrates in the Chengjiang formation, this small, basal fish lived about 525 million years ago, in the Early Cambrian Epoch. *Myllokunmingia* coexisted with trilobites, ancient shrimplike arthropods, fossil worms, and large, free-swimming predatory anomalocarids that measured several feet in length. *Myllokunmingia* measured only about an inch long (28 mm). The much-celebrated discovery of *Myllokunmingia* was followed by the finding of more than 500 additional specimens, thereby providing a wealth of information about this early vertebrate.

As the earliest known jawless fish, *Myllokunmingia* shared many of the traits that are seen in the better-known jawless fishes of the Ordovician and Silurian Periods. *Myllokunmingia* had a distinctly fishlike, elongate body with a tapered head. The dorsal and ventral sides of the animal were adorned with long lateral fins, and the tail was equipped with a single, unpaired fin. A sequence of 24 V-shaped muscle bands extended along most of the length of the body. There is little trace of hard parts, and there is certainly no bony skeleton, suggesting that *Myllokunmingia* had an internal skeleton made of cartilage. In most cases, cartilage totally decays before an animal becomes fossilized, but traces in the form of stains and impressions are sometimes left behind. Some specimens of *Myllokunmingia* show the presence of a riblike "basket" extending laterally down from the back of the animal in the form of 25 paired arches, perhaps a preservational remnant or stain associated with a cartilaginous skeleton. There are at least six gill slits running along the side of the anterior end of the body. The head is clearly defined as a region of darker preservation, including two blackish spots that might represent a pair of eyes. The darker color of the head of *Myllokunmingia* may also suggest that its anterior was protected by a harder outer covering. Such bony armor is more evident in later jawless fishes.

In 2003, Degan Shu and his colleagues identified one more primitive vertebrate from the fauna of the Early Cambrian Chengjiang Formation. This was an eel-like creature named *Zhongjianichthys*

Myllokunmingia—the first known vertebrate—was a jawless fish.

that clearly showed evidence of riblike vertebral arches and a pair of eyes.

Myllokunmingia and *Zhongjianichthys* are more than a mere foreshadowing of things to come in fishes. These two early vertebrates prove that a remarkable evolutionary backstory was taking place in the midst of the Cambrian invertebrate explosion of life. These two tiny vertebrate fishes—exhibiting gills, fins, notochords, paired eyes, and elongate cartilaginous skeletons—shed light on the early history of fishes that otherwise were known only from the patchiest of evidence.

The Conodonta

Another long-lived group of early vertebrates was the conodonts, a taxon that was largely a mystery for more than 125 years because the remains of these creatures consisted only of tiny, toothlike structures made of calcium phosphate. These structures were presumably held together in life by soft tissue that was not preserved in the fossil record. The presence of calcium phosphate structures alone was a tantalizing hint that the conodonts possessed hard parts made of materials found only in vertebrates, but nothing else was known to help scientists draw a more complete picture of these creatures. Even the most enigmatic fossils may prove important to paleontology if found in great enough numbers, however. In the case of the conodonts, their tiny parts are so varied and abundant in marine deposits ranging from Middle Cambrian to Triassic times that they are used as an **index fossil** for dating stratigraphic layers.

The name conodont most accurately refers to the denticle structures that once were part of the feeding apparatus of these animals, although the name is used synonymously for the animal itself. Conodonts are classified as the Conodonta, a primitive subclass of jawless fishes. Conodonts first appear in fossil records from the Middle Cambrian Epoch, which positions them in time between the rise of the first vertebrates, such as *Myllokunmingia,* and the dramatic rise of the better-known fishes from the Ordovician Period.

Toothlike conodont structures are found in dozens of forms. Some consist of isolated conical points and stubs; others are attached to a jawlike substrate that resembles combs and crustacean claws. All are tiny and require a microscope to examine closely.

The fact that no complete specimen of a conodont creature had been found in more than 125 years of looking did not discourage some imaginative paleontologists from trying to reconstruct an image of these animals. Most interpretations began with an attempt to understand how the toothlike structures operated. This itself was challenging because the parts were complex in form and jumbled together from having become disassembled during the decay of the animals. Making matters even more challenging for the paleontologist was the minute size of conodont remains; these tiny denticles are barely visible to the naked eye and require magnification under a microscope. Interpreting how conodont feeding mechanisms functioned in life was akin to trying to assemble a power drill from a pile of its loose parts.

If one assumed that the conodont fossils were in fact part of a feeding mechanism—a detail that at one time was disputed by some scientists—it was clear that these were not jaws like those normally seen in later vertebrates. Some paleontologists pictured the conodont tooth apparatus covered by a membrane to facilitate filter feeding. Others invented a variety of possible assemblages of the tooth structures for grasping, sawing, chopping, and shredding prey. Had a complete specimen of a conodont been found, the job of interpreting its feeding mechanism would have been somewhat easier. Lacking such a specimen, some conodont experts attempted to picture the form of these creatures despite a paucity of physical evidence. One of the most creative was Swedish conodont expert Maurits Lindström (b. 1932), who, in the 1960s, pictured the conodont as a bloated, filter-feeding donut with spikes.

The true nature of the animals that carried these toothlike structures was unknown until 1983, when the complete specimen *Clydagnathus* was discovered. Found in rocks of Early Carboniferous age in Edinburgh, Scotland, the fossil likeness was a mere streak among many fossils of invertebrates that included extinct shrimplike arthropods. Invertebrate paleontologists Euan Clarkson (b. 1937) and Derek Briggs (b. 1950) then best known for their studies of Paleozoic invertebrates, noticed the conodont specimen among slabs of shale that they were studying at the Royal Scottish Museum. Had they not been interested in the shrimplike fossils adjacent to the conodont, it may never have been discovered. The creature had an eel-like body that was a slight 1.6 inches (40.5 mm) long. Examination under a microscope revealed that the specimen had a group of conodont denticles collected at one end of the body. Because Clarkson and Briggs were experts on arthropods rather than conodonts, the two scientists called in acquaintance Richard Aldridge (b. 1945), a dedicated conodont specialist. One look through the microscope convinced Aldridge that he had in fact come face to face with the first known body fossil of a conodont. The mysterious feeding mechanism could be seen in place in the oral cavity of the head region.

Conodont structures

Toothlike conodont structures are so small that they can rest on the head of a pin.

This first discovery of a conodont body fossil in Scotland was followed by others in Scotland and South Africa. This startling evidence provided paleontologists with convincing clues to the vertebrate affinity of these early creatures. The eel-like body was clearly bilateral and appeared to house a notochord laterally along its back. The conodont form was also composed of V-shaped muscle groups—the bands of muscles found in similar vertebrates that enabled the animals to wiggle their bodies and swim. The presence of a clearly defined head and pharynx region and paired eyes also fit with the traits associated with vertebrates. The presence of cellular bone among fossilized conodont elements was confirmed in 1992 by a team of British paleontologists at the University of Durham.

One new conodont species called *Promissum* was originally mistaken for a plant until Richard Aldridge investigated it. In 1990, Aldridge confirmed that this organism was in fact a giant among conodonts. The name *Promissum* remained, even though the organism was no longer considered a plant. Found in Late Ordovician sediments in South Africa, *Promissum* measured 16 inches (40 cm) long. Additional specimens described in 1994 and 1995 clearly confirmed the presence of a pair of eyes on the head of this conodont.

Having several specimens of conodont body fossils in hand also led to better informed attempts to explain how the feeding mechanism worked. Two colleagues of Aldridge, British paleontologists Mark A. Purnell (b. 1964) and Philip C.J. Donoghue (b. 1971) of the University of Leicester, produced the best-researched and most comprehensive interpretation of this puzzling aspect of conodont anatomy. In 1997, the pair published an extensive study using three-dimensional modeling that showed the most likely mechanics behind one of the most complex conodont forms, that of the species *Idiognathodus*. This species is known only from fossils of its feeding mechanism from Late Carboniferous rocks of Illinois. After experimenting with several different arrangements of the feeding mechanism parts, Purnell and Donoghue favored an elaborate design that gave these tiny animals a formidable tool for capturing, dicing, and swallowing tiny prey. Long rows of spiky denticles were drawn back and up to grasp prey and draw it into the mouth area. The teeth were pointed backward to prevent prey from wriggling loose. After the creature grasped the food in these denticles, the serrated tooth elements would slice and chop the food like serrated scissors by turning and scraping against one another. Further supporting this model of the conodont feeding mechanism were microimages taken by Purnell that showed wear patterns on the surface of the denticles. This additional evidence not only shows that these conodont structures were indeed teeth, but also suggests that the first vertebrates were predators.

The diet of conodonts can be implied from the design of their feeding contraptions. "There is no direct evidence in the form of gut contents for the conodont diet," explained Aldridge in correspondence with this author. "But microwear patterns on a number of conodont specimens show that at least some normal-sized conodonts ate resistant food, probably zooplankton [microscopic animals suspended in ocean water]. Functional considerations indicate that conodonts were ***macrophagous*** [predators and/or **scavengers**] on small prey," rather than being filter feeders of phytoplankton [unicellular algae suspended in ocean water].

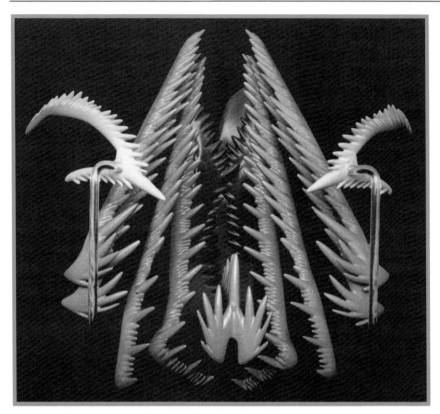

Mark Purnell's computer model of a conodont jaw

The evolutionary position of the conodonts is apparently unrelated to vertebrates that followed. Although the conodonts exhibit some of the characteristics of later fishes, including the presence of cellular bone, a bilateral body plan, a pair of eyes, and a notochord, their feeding apparatus remains unique in the animal **kingdom**. Based on current evidence, it is doubtful that conodonts were in the direct line of ascent to the plentiful families of fishes that rose later. The Conodonta were more likely fantastically successful taxa that evolved in parallel with fishes prior to becoming extinct in the Triassic Period. Somewhere deeper in the past, at the base of the vertebrate family tree, is a common ancestor of all vertebrates that has yet to be discovered.

VERTEBRATES OVER TIME: THE BIG PICTURE

All 10 major fish groups have roots in the Ordovician Period, and spectacular fossils of many kinds of extinct fishes become widely abundant during the Silurian and Devonian Periods. Fishes of many kinds also survived the Permian-Triassic extinction, tipping the evolutionary balance in favor of the vertebrates that soon would dominate Earth's ecosystems on land and sea.

Vertebrates first evolved in the Paleozoic oceans; this evolution led to the diversity of animals that are collectively known as fishes. From the fishes sprang the amphibians that in turn led to the reptiles, birds, and mammals. The relative success of these different groups of vertebrates has been tempered over time by changes to worldwide habitats, competition among the creatures themselves, and the effects of extinction events. The peak of amphibian success, for example, occurred during the Carboniferous and Permian Periods, when vast rain forests made up the broad equatorial regions of Paleozoic landmasses. The amphibians' dominance dwindled at the end of the Paleozoic Era for at least two reasons. The events that caused the Permian-Triassic mass extinction included widespread climate changes that shrank the vast, moist coal forests that amphibians needed to survive. At the same time, another type of vertebrate was on the rise—a type that was more adaptable to differing climate conditions: the reptile. In a like manner, the rise of modern bony fishes may have been kept on hold during most of the Paleozoic because of competition from earlier jawed fishes including spiny sharks, placoderms, and cartilaginous fishes. The ranks of bony fishes rose dramatically beginning in the Early Mesozoic Era. The bony fishes rapidly grew in diversity and number and remain the longest surviving jawed vertebrates. The history of the vertebrates demonstrates a remarkable progression of adaptive features over time.

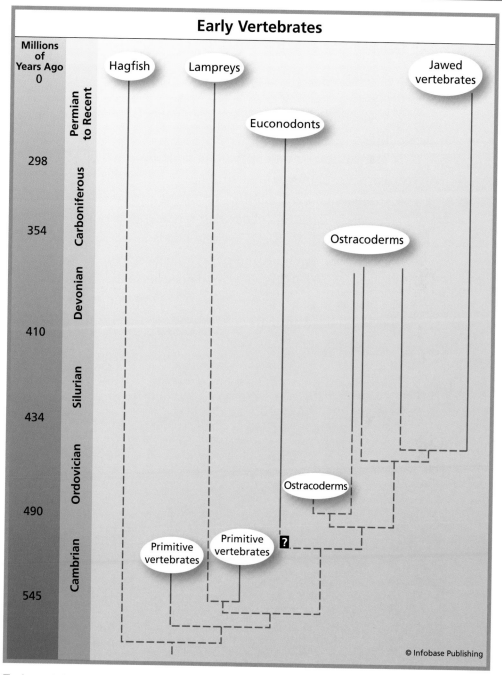

Early vertebrate evolution

SUMMARY

This chapter discussed the origins of the first vertebrates.

1. Among the earliest chordates were the eel-like cephalochordates.
2. Vertebrates first evolved in the Cambrian oceans as jawless fishes.
3. The earliest known vertebrate is *Myllokunmingia,* from the Early Cambrian of China.
4. Conodonts were another group of early vertebrates from the early Paleozoic. They had a bilateral, eel-like body with a notochord, V-shaped muscle bands along the body, and a clearly defined head and pharynx region with paired eyes.
5. The first vertebrates were predatory animals.
6. The rise of fishes in the Paleozoic oceans led to the diversity of backboned animals on land and sea that included the evolution of amphibians, reptiles, mammals, and birds.

SECTION THREE:
THE RISE OF THE FISHES

5

JAWLESS FISHES

Following the origin of early fishes—the first vertebrates—in the Cambrian Period, the evolution of fishes underwent several dramatic **developmental** episodes. These episodes were marked by the appearance of many diverse groups, extinctions, and success stories. Fishes—the most long-standing and successful group of vertebrates—were also the stock from which land animals evolved later in the Paleozoic Era.

It is assumed that the group of early fishes known as the Agnatha evolved from a single ancestor. Because the class Agnatha probably does not include all of the descendants of that ancestor, however, the evolutionary relationships between different clans of jawless fishes are not understood. All other fishes are members of the group Gnathostomata, which includes all jawed vertebrates, fish or otherwise. Classes of jawed fishes within the **gnathostomes**, living and extinct, include the Placodermi ("flat-plated skins"); Chondrichthyes (cartilaginous fishes); Acanthodii ("spiny sharks"); and Osteichthyes (bony fishes). The rise of the jawless fishes from the Late Cambrian Epoch and Ordovician Period to the close of the Devonian Period (488 million to 359 million years ago) is the subject of this chapter.

TRAITS OF JAWLESS FISHES

As seen in Chapter 4, the fossil record of basal jawless fishes of the Cambrian Period is relatively spotty except for the surprisingly good evidence for a select few, including *Myllokunmingia*, *Zhongjianichthys*, *Clydagnathus* and *Promissum*. The fossil record of the Ordovician is equally stingy, consisting primarily of one taxon known primarily from patches of body armor and two spectacular jawless fishes from late in the period. Other suspected fishes from the Ordovician are known from little more than fragmentary pieces of body armor and scales. Not until the fossil record of the Silurian and Devonian Periods do significant body fossils of many kinds of early fishes become apparent.

As of yet, there is a lack of definitive fossils to document an evolutionary transition between the first Cambrian vertebrates and the agnathans of the later Paleozoic. What we do know is this: Sometime during the 80 million years between the rise of the earliest, eel-like vertebrates and the Late Ordovician Epoch, an entirely new kind of animal had begun to populate the oceans. Instead of having a slight and sliverlike body that wriggled through the ocean currents, this creature was an armored plated, finless torpedo that probably dwelled near the ocean floor, sucking up sediment for scraps of food. One such fish was *Astraspis*.

These distinct clans of jawless fishes shared several characteristics. Instead of having jaws—a hallmark feature of later vertebrates—agnathans had simple mouth openings that they used to dredge up food from silt or capture floating organisms in the water as they swam. The agnathans' skeletons were cartilaginous, composed of gristle, and so left behind little fossil evidence of the creatures' internal body structure. Jawless fish bodies were protected by an array of bony armor plates, or scales, or both. Most agnathans had no fins and only a simple tail that could be wagged back and forth. Agnathans had paired eyes in the head region, usually to the sides or just above the mouth cavity.

Agnathans were small creatures; the largest types averaged only about 12 inches (30 cm) long. Jawless fishes were mere "small fry" in the waters of the Middle Paleozoic, which left no question as to the need for protective outer armor. Agnathans had to guard against significantly larger invertebrate predators, including "water scorpions" (eurypterids) and crustaceans, some of which reached lengths of nine feet (2.5 m).

Even with their variety of body shapes and outer coverings, this collection of early vertebrates succeeded in building, generation after generation, taxon after taxon, a general direction for the body plan of animals with backbones. The head became increasingly defined as an important part of the anatomy. Encapsulated in protective outer bony plates, the brain of these early fishes began to increase in size over the millennia of their evolution. The bilateral symmetry of agnathans resulted in a well-defined body plan with a sense of direction: Forward and backward motion were relative to the anterior (head) and posterior (tail) ends of the animal. The jawless fishes' bodies could also be described as having upper and lower surfaces and sides. Jawless fishes swam in one direction, head first, propelled by a tail. Eyes at the front, adjacent to the mouth, enabled jawless fishes to effectively locate and sweep food into their suckerlike mouths. Taken as a whole, these anatomical developments were gradually perfecting the status of jawless fishes as cautious background predators that combined a mobile body plan with sharp senses, nerve structures, and the acumen needed to compete successfully for food in the living ocean.

The fact that most jawless fishes were extinct by the end of the Devonian Period is a testament to the benefit of having jaws: the ability to grasp and consume a wider variety of prey more efficiently. Although agnathans were highly successful for many millions of years, they found it difficult to compete once their toothed brethren had diversified. The only living descendants of agnathans are lampreys and hagfishes, two varieties of eel-shaped parasites that hitch rides on larger fish. The ancestors of these living relics found a niche for themselves that was unoccupied by jawed fishes, adapting over time to the life of a parasite. A lamprey latches onto a host using a tonguelike appendage equipped with prickly teeth and then sucks the host's blood or slowly eats its flesh. The agnathan *Jamoytius*, found in Silurian deposits, was quite similar in form to the modern lamprey. Although *Jamoytius* was probably not a parasite, it had an elongate body with a pair of laterally placed, forward-facing eyes, small rows of gill holes behind the eyes, and vertically oriented fins running along the top and bottom of its body. This tubelike creature appeared to have suckers for a mouth and may have been an early line of agnathans leading to the modern lampreys.

SUBGROUPS OF JAWLESS FISHES

As a class, the Agnatha include the living lampreys and hagfishes. They also include a number of extinct groups, including Myllokunmingiida and Conodonta; the Astraspida, Arandaspida, Heterostraci, Anaspida, and Thelodonti; and the Osteostraci, Galeaspida, and Pituriaspids.

Anatolepis

Aside from the exquisite examples of early vertebrates, fossils of other jawless fishes from the Cambrian and Ordovician Periods are extremely rare and fragmentary. Prior to the discovery in China of *Myllokunmingia* and other early vertebrates from the Early Cambrian, the most provocative fossil of an early vertebrate had been a scrappy specimen known as *Anatolepis*. Found in Spitzbergen, Norway, the fossils were described in 1976 by paleontologists Tove G. Bockelie and Richard Fortey (b. 1946). While examining marine deposits for microfossils, the two paleontologists were surprised to find what appeared to be tiny scales. The specimens were miniscule, ranging from a mere 0.39 to 0.78 inches (1 to 2 mm) long. Closer examination revealed that the specimens consisted of small sections of scales attached to pieces of hard dermal skin. The microscope also revealed tiny porous channels, which the scientists interpreted as being evidence of apatite, along with spaces for nerves or blood vessels. Since its discovery, additional specimens of *Anatolepis* have been found in sedimentary rocks dating from the Late Cambrian to Early Ordovician in North America, Greenland, Norway, and Australia. A reexamination of all available *Anatolepis* specimens in 1996 established that the dermal material contained dentine, a hard tissue unique to vertebrates.

There is not enough evidence to describe the appearance of *Anatolepis*. The small size of the scales suggests an equally tiny

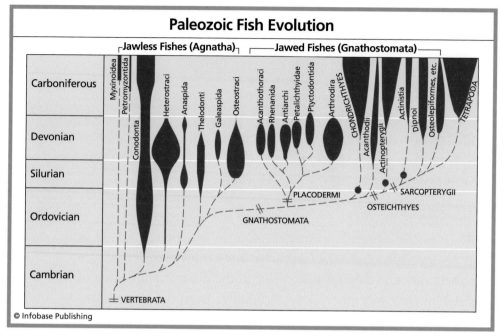

Paleozoic Fish Evolution

Evolution and diversification of early fishes

fish, probably only a few inches long. When Bockelie and Fortey first described it, they considered *Anatolepis* to be a heterostracan, a member of the first widely diverse group of fishes. Even with the affinity of *Anatolepis* in doubt, however, its existence shows that this fish appeared around the same time as the first conodonts. This indicates that the development of early vertebrates was well under way in several directions by the start of the Ordovician Period.

Astraspida and Arandaspida

While fragmentary fossil evidence—mostly pieces of dermal armor—is generally the rule for Ordovician jawless fishes, there are a few eye-opening exceptions. The most spectacular of these specimens have been classed as members of the taxa Arandaspida and Astraspida and consist of several dazzling examples.

The astraspids are represented by the lone taxon *Astraspis,* from the Harding Sandstone formation of Colorado. Charles Walcott

(1850–1927) discovered the first specimen in 1892. This was the same man who in 1909 identified the marvelous Cambrian fossil beds of the Burgess Shale in western Canada.

Astraspis lived during the Middle Ordovician Epoch, about 450 million years ago. The best *Astraspis* specimens have been discovered in Colorado, although the creature is also known from specimens found in Arizona, Oklahoma, Wyoming, and Quebec, Canada. Measuring no more than 8 inches (20 cm) long, *Astraspis* was adorned with vaguely star-shaped bony plates—the source of its name, which translates to "star shield." The head of *Astraspis* was heavily armored by a shield of tilelike plates. *Astraspis* had two large eyes positioned on the sides of its head. A small armored ringlet of bony tubercules protected each eye. A sequence of eight branched gill openings ran laterally on each side of the head. The head armor ended about midway down the length of the body, at which point the back end of *Astraspis* was covered by a matrix of small (and more flexible) diamond-shaped scales. The creature's tail is not well known from its fossils but is thought probably to have consisted of a single, vertically oriented fin that the animal waved from side to side to propel itself. The body of *Astraspis* lacked fins of any other kind, making it a clumsy swimmer at best.

The Arandaspida are known from four genera, the best examples of which are *Arandaspis,* from Early Ordovician rocks in Australia, and *Sacabambaspis,* from Late Ordovician deposits in Bolivia. Arandaspids were also small; they measured between 6 and 8 inches (15 and 20 cm) long and superficially resemble the projectile-shaped astraspids. The details of the arandaspids' body armor differ significantly from the armor plating of their North American relatives, however.

The arandaspids did not have a head shield composed of many smaller, tilelike plates. Instead, the upper and lower armored head plates of an arandaspid consisted of a one-piece, ornamented shield coupled with one or more bony straps on the sides of the head. The midline of the upper plate was ridged down the middle, and the bottom plate dipped down into a deep, bowl-like shape. Rather than having exposed gill holes, as did *Astraspis*, the arandaspids had gills that were covered by a bony grille. The eyes of the arandaspids *Arandaspis* and *Sacabambaspis* were farther forward than the eyes of *Astraspis* and, in the case of *Sacabambaspis*, perched clearly on the anterior end of the body. The back half of the arandaspid body was covered by strips of bony armor rather than by small scales.

Specimens of astraspids and arandaspids, although few in number, fill some important gaps in the fossil record of early fishes. Being poor swimmers, these fish probably stayed close to calm waters near the bottom of shallow seabeds and scooped up detritus and other organic material from silt and the water through which they wriggled. A study of arandaspid dermal armor published in 2005 by Ivan J. Sansom, Philip C.J. Donoghue, and Guillermo Albanesi revealed that the bony armor of these creatures was partly composed of apatite in the form of dentine and enamel. This provided additional evidence that these early vertebrates were part of a lineage that also included the most abundant group of jawless fishes, the Heterostraci.

Heterostraci

One of the most diverse and abundant groups of agnathans is from the order Heterostraci. Numbering about 300 species, the heterostracans thrived from the Early Silurian to the Late Devonian Epoch (430 million to 370 million years ago). Heterostracans have been found in such widespread Northern Hemisphere fossil localities as North America, Greenland, Great Britain, Germany, Norway, Belgium, Siberia, and China.

Like the astraspids and arandaspids, the heterostracans possessed a head shield that consisted of large upper and lower plates and one or more smaller plates on the sides of the head. The head armor was composed of dentine and noncellular bone and was sometimes ornamented with sharp spines and ridges that ran lengthwise along the body. The armor on the side of the head had holes for gill openings. The armor plating of the head could grow as the animal got older and larger. Heterostracans were generally small. They measured between 6 and 12 inches (15 and 30 cm) long except for one group with a paddle-shaped body that measured up to 3.33 feet (1 m) long and 50 inches (1.5 m) wide.

Heterostracans had little more than a tail fin to propel their heavily armored bodies through the water, so swimming did not come easy for them. Except for a few members of the group, most heterostracans had about as much maneuverability as giant tadpoles wrapped in chain mail. Heterostracans were most likely bottom dwellers, taking in free-floating organisms along the sandy bottoms of near-shore marine environments and freshwater lakes and streams. Despite many similarities with the astraspids and arandaspids, the heterostracans were distinguished from them by having several unique variations in the shape and size of the head armor and by having single, rather than multiple, gill holes on either side of the head for respiration.

Even with their design limitations, heterostracans were a long-lived **clade** of vertebrates. The heterostracans spanned the Silurian and Devonian Periods and reached their peak of diversity during the Late Silurian and Early Devonian. The simplicity of their form relied on external armor for protection, single gill openings that minimized the number of invasive openings to their bodies, and jawless, suckerlike mouths defined by a bony ridge that helped scrape up food from the seafloor.

Heterostracans fall into four groups: the cyathaspids, the amphiaspids, the pteraspids, and the psammosteids.

The cyathaspids had a long body that was entirely covered with armor plates. The head was protected by large, single dorsal and ventral plates. The gill openings were shielded by a bony strip on the side of the head. Behind the head shield, the entire cyathaspid body was covered by overlapping rows of diamond-shaped plates and scales that somewhat resembled modern fish or reptile scales. The cyathaspid tail, as seen in the species *Athenaegis*, was vertically oriented and could be wagged from side to side. The jawless, suckerlike mouth was quipped with a fanlike lower plate and bony upper plate. These jawless fish had a streamlined body but no fins of any kind.

Model of the cyathaspid *Athenaegis*

This had led to speculation that they may have propelled themselves by spurting out jets of water from their gill openings. The cyathaspids were one of the longest surviving groups of heterostracans; they thrived from the Late Silurian to the Early Devonian.

The amphiaspids were not around as long as the cyathaspids. Amphiaspids have been found only in rocks that date from the Early Devonian Epoch. Specimens from Siberia show that the amphiaspid head was entirely encased in a solid armor shield. The tail was vertically oriented, with a fin divided into rays by several tapered rows of scales. Because amphiaspids such as *Ctenaspis* and *Eglonaspis* had smaller eyes than other heterostracans and what appeared to be a branchial opening (a gill opening) on top of the head shield, it is thought that these fishes may have lived half-buried in bottom sediment. Completing the picture of this sedentary feeder was a bony tube that led to the jawless mouth. Presumably, an amphiaspid such as *Ctenaspis* lay half buried in the mud, unable to see but able to breathe and suck planktonic food through a bony mouth tube that protruded upward.

The pteraspids lived from the Early to Middle Devonian and are represented by many good specimens. In these jawless fishes, the dorsal head shield was composed of several separate plates that varied widely in shape and size. Hind scales on the body were smaller than those of the cyathaspids, and the body was sometimes adorned with spines and sharp ridges on the top and sides. Tails varied among the many species of pteraspids. Pteraspid tails had two or three vertically oriented joined fins that could be moved from side to side. In some species, such as *Pteraspis*, the bottom tail fin was markedly longer than the top fin. Notably, there were several reinforced bony structures of the head, including plates around the eyes, the branchial opening, the mouth, and a long, pointed, snoutlike rostrum (projection). Behind the head shield, the rear of the pteraspid body was covered with smaller scales that resembled those of modern fish. This suggests that the fanlike tail could be swung back and forth by a muscular body. The combination of a powerful tail with bony, winglike side fenders made the pteraspids more maneuverable than other heterostracans. Assuming that these fish were decent swimmers, the pteraspids probably roamed in moderately deep water to feed on planktonic animals suspended in the water.

The large and paddle-shaped psammosteids were a departure in many ways from other heterostracans. In cross section, the psammosteids resembled rays with a bony outer covering. The psammosteids' bodies were flat; this made them well suited for scavenging through mud for food. The psammosteid head had a more complex matrix of shield plates and scales than the heads of other heterostracans. On top was a bony cap surrounded by rows of smaller, scalelike plates. Separate bony plates protected the eyes, the gills, and the mouth area. The sides of these fishes were covered by scalelike rows of dermal armor; these joined with a belly plate equipped with a yachtlike keel. The side gill openings were protected by a bony

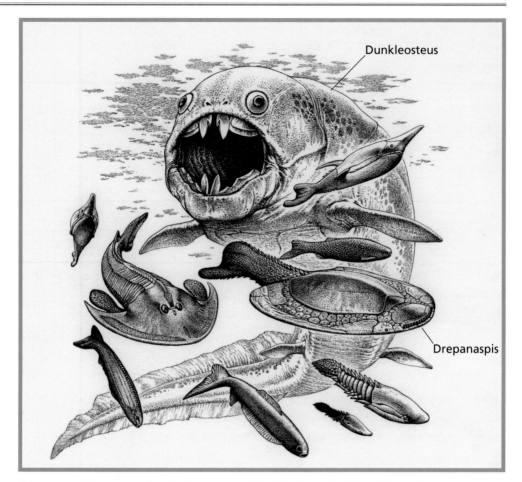

A large predator swimming by the armor-plated bottom dwelling Heterostracan *Drepanaspis*

channel reminiscent of the exhaust pipe on an automobile. To the rear of the psammosteid body was a scaly tail with web-shaped fins that could be waved up and down. The largest of these creatures, represented by *Drepanaspis*, reached lengths of 3.33 feet (1 m). The eyes of *Drepanaspis* were spread wide apart.

Anaspida

Two outlying groups of jawless fishes whose evolutionary relationship with other agnathans is not entirely understood were the anaspids and thelodonts. Both groups had less body armor than other jawless fishes, particularly around the head. Without much armor, their fragile skeletons were not readily fossilized.

Anaspids were small- to medium-sized jawless fishes; they measured from 4 to 11 inches (10 to 27 cm) long. The body plan of such anaspids as *Pharyngolepis* and *Pterygolepis* was more reminiscent of modern fish than was the body plan of other agnathans. Anaspids had a long, slender body that was shaped somewhat like a tube flattened inward from the sides. The head region was made up of a large, round mouth opening at the anterior; small eyes on the sides of the head; and a row of 6 to 15 small gill openings that slanted downward behind the eyes. Just behind these branchial openings was a spiny point that is found in all anaspids. Although these fishes had no fins on the upper side of the body, most had one small fin on the bottom, near the anal opening. A long, finlike fold ran along each side of the body from behind the gill openings to the tail. These side fins were not stiff or muscled, so they did not serve as stabilizers while the fish were swimming. Paired tail fins rose vertically along a downwardly pointed tail. At least one taxon of advanced anaspids, *Rhyncholepis*, had paired fins about midway along the belly side, just behind the head region. This was a foreshadowing of anatomical improvement in later jawless fishes and resembles somewhat the design of modern lampreys, to which it is thought the anaspids might be ancestral.

The anaspid body was covered with long, thin scales that formed a chevron pattern (∧). These scales might disclose the location of segmented muscles that would have helped these fishes to wriggle through the water. Because the anaspids lacked dorsal fins and strong side fins, however, they probably were poor swimmers.

The best known anaspids lived during a relatively short span of the Late Silurian (430 million to 410 million years ago), but some possible members of this group have been found in Late Devonian deposits. The most complete anaspid specimens, including whole body impressions, have been found in Silurian deposits in Norway and Scotland. The anaspids thrived in marine coastal habitats of Europe and North America and also made their way into fresh waters.

Thelodonti

Because the thelodonts lacked outer bony armor, they are known primarily from one common physical feature that they left behind: tiny, thick dermal scales that measure about 0.39 inches (1 mm) long. The design of the scales is distinctive; they have a round or oval shape with a ringlike edge and a pulp cavity. A few, rare body fossils such as that of *Archipelepis,* from the Silurian of Arctic Canada, show that the thelodonts had the general body plan of other fish. The elongate body was somewhat flattened and covered by its characteristic scales. Body armor was completely absent. The anterior mouth opening was round and large, there were two small eyes on the sides of the head, and eight gill slits ran along the side of the head beneath a bony flap. The thelodonts also had small, finlike flaps on the dorsal and ventral surfaces near the base of the tail. The tail fin was long and projected downward.

One unusual group of thelodonts, including *Furcacauda* from the Silurian and Devonian of the Canadian Northwest Territories, broke the thelodont mold by having a tall, deep body that was flattened vertically. This gave *Furcacauda* a humpbacked profile. *Furcacauda* also had large eyes and a large, nearly symmetrical forked tail. Most interesting, perhaps, is evidence for the presence of a stomach in these Canadian thelodonts, an anatomical feature previously thought to have evolved later with the coming of true jaws.

Thelodonts were small; they averaged about 7 inches (18 cm) long. The earliest scales are found in the Middle to Late Ordovician Epochs, but specimens of the entire body have been restricted to younger deposits ranging from the Early Silurian to the Late Devonian (430 million to 370 million years ago).

Osteostraci, Galeaspida, and Pituriaspida

The last stage of the great radiation of jawless fishes was dominated by three groups that were known for their massive head shields. All three clades—the osteostracans, the galeaspids, and the pituriaspids—had large, bony head armor that covered the gill openings. Unlike the head shields of the heterostracans, which were composed of individual plates that could expand as the animal grew larger, the head armor of these three groups of agnathans was not jointed and could not grow.

There were more than 200 species of osteostracans. They are found in fossil beds that date from the Early Silurian to the Late Devonian (430 million to 370 million years ago) and are widely distributed in the Northern Hemisphere: in North America, Europe, Siberia, and Central Asia. Osteostracans ranged widely in size, from a tiny 1.5 inches (4 cm) to a gigantic 3.33 feet (1 m) long. Most averaged between 8 and 16 inches (20 and 40 cm) in length.

The body of an osteostracan was wide and flat-bottomed; it was well adapted for bottom feeding. The shape and curvature of the head shield was somewhat like that of the modern horseshoe crab. The osteostracan head was composed of one bony, protective piece with two closely spaced holes for eyes that were largely aimed upward. The body behind the head shield was covered by large scales.

The head shields of osteostracans were highly ornamented and varied from species to species. The armor of *Hemicyclaspis* was relatively simple; it consisted of a simple, curved semicircular piece of bone that resembled a knee pad used by in-line skaters. Other species were adorned with increasingly distinctive shields. Some shields got broader and deeper; others formed sharp spines at the side of the head; several had backward-pointing bony wings that protected the gills. At least two species developed highly elongated rostrums.

Osteostracans were possibly the most advanced of the jawless vertebrates and had many affinities with the jawed fishes that followed. Most significantly, osteostracans were the first jawless fishes to have true, paired pectoral fins. Positioned on the sides of the animal, just behind the head shield, these appendages may have been the forerunners of modern fins on fishes—and the precursors of

(continues on page 96)

THINK ABOUT IT

The Old Red Sandstone of Scotland:
Hugh Miller and the Popularization of Science

One of the most abundant sources of fossil Devonian jawless fishes, placoderms, acanthodians, and lobe-finned fishes is the Old Red Sandstone formation of northern Scotland. This area, rich in fossil deposits, was once the site of an expansive subtropical lake. A periodic cycle of natural fish kills in that lake is now revealed by thousands of fish fossils laid bare in various red sandstone deposits across various parts of Scotland.

Chemical analysis of the deposits suggests that the fish kills occurred during times when the oxygen content of the lake was at dangerously low levels—levels that literally suffocated many of the lake's fish inhabitants. Anoxic events of this kind can occur during a severe bloom of lake algae. The same effect can occur when the anoxic deep waters of such a lake are stirred to the top, perhaps as a result of a violent storm or tectonic event. Whatever the cause, it seems that about every 10 years, a large number of the lake's inhabitants died off, floated to the middle of the lake, and then sank into the deepest, anoxic waters, where they became covered by fine sediment. Because the carcasses were so deep in the lake, where the oxygen content was so low, they were spared from being scavenged. This left many of their skeletons wholly intact. Over several thousands of years, many layers of fossils built up on the lake bottom, laminated in thin layers of mud and stacked with intervening layers of sandstone that lacked fossils. Eventually, the layers built up to thicknesses of up to 33 feet (10 m). The Old Red Sandstone gets its name from the rusty color of the sediments.

Hugh Miller was a Scottish stonemason, amateur geologist, and poet who opposed the idea that life-forms evolved over time to generate new species. Miller scoured areas near his home for fossils and collected a vast number. Miller did not believe that humans evolved from earlier, ancestral life-forms. Restricting his observations to the fossil fauna of the Scottish red sandstone, Miller was unable to see obvious connections between earlier forms of life and later ones. He stated at one point that "the early fossils ought to be very small in size" and "very low in organization." He expected to see simpler and smaller life-forms in the earlier strata and larger, more complex ones in the later strata. Instead, Miller found a diverse assemblage of fishes of many shapes and sizes in all strata. This led him to believe in the theory of "special creation"—the theory that God created life in several consecutive efforts, with each effort concluded by a mass extinction that wiped the slate clean. Miller's studies of fossil formations and his interest in geology, however, allowed him

Hugh Miller

a broader, scientific view of some of the other issues that confounded nonscientists. He believed that organisms could become extinct. He also believed that the age of the Earth was geologically vast and that there is no geologic proof for a global flood such as that recounted in the story of Noah in the Bible.

Equipped with a poetic style of rhetoric and a persuasive personality, Miller aimed his own writing at a popular audience. His most famous book, *The Old Red Sandstone*, was published in 1841. The book provided the public with an imaginative view of fossils and their origins, making it one of the most important early works to popularize the sciences of geology and paleontology. Miller ably mixed scientific description with metaphysical musings.

(continues)

(continued)

By the mid-1850s, the stonemason poet had become a popular speaker on subjects related to religion and the fossil record. Unfortunately, Miller's health deteriorated, as evidenced by severe headaches and apparent bouts of depression and hallucinations that the doctors of his day were unable to diagnose. Miller died in 1856, after completing the last of his works to be published. Miller's extraordinary collection of Devonian fossils and his inspired style of discourse influenced many people to take an interest in science and examine the natural world as revealed by geology and fossils.

(continued from page 93)

paired limbs in land vertebrates. Some osteostracans, such as *Hemicyclaspis*, also had a single dorsal fin placed far along the back and a large, upward-pointing lobe on the tail. This tail design differed from most other jawless fishes, which had down-turned tails. The upward-pointing tail enabled *Hemicyclaspis* to keep its body pointed toward the seafloor, a terrific adaptation for a bottom-feeding fish. When considered as a working unit, the pectoral flaps, dorsal fin, and tail made the osteostracans some of the most capable swimmers among the agnathans.

Another important aspect of heterostracan anatomy was that these fishes were one of the first vertebrates to show evidence of a bony skeleton. As an osteostracan grew, bone was laid down inside its body over the surface of the cartilaginous skeleton. Bone will fossilize whereas cartilage will not, so specimens of osteostracans provide some of the earliest clues to the internal anatomy of the vertebrates. The detail inside the fossilized head shield is so fine in some fossil specimens that it provides a clear picture of the nerve connections and sensory functions of these jawless fish.

Like the osteostracans, the galeaspids had an oversized head shield in which both the endoskeleton and exoskeleton contained bone. The front of the shield contained a large opening on the upper surface, probably for respiration. Behind the head shield, the body was protected by smaller scales arranged in rows. Galeaspids differed significantly from osteostracans in that the galeaspids lacked paired side fins and had no dorsal fins. The galeaspids' head shields were in some ways even more distinctive than those of the osteostracans. The shields of the galeaspids took on square and triangular forms, had elongated rostrums, and had long spiny rostrums on the sides. Fossils of galeaspids are found in deposits from the Silurian and Devonian Periods in southern China and Vietnam.

The pituriaspids are known only from two fragmentary species found in Early Devonian deposits in Queensland, Australia: *Pituriaspis* and *Neeyambaspis*. The only trait that clearly distinguishes these incomplete specimens from the osteostracans and galeaspids is a large pit found on the upper surface of the head shield just below the eyes.

THE LABORATORY OF EARLY FISHES

The agnathans were the first successful vertebrates, yet this experiment in the evolution of backboned animals sputtered to a close by the middle of the Paleozoic as more advanced fishes grew in abundance and sophistication. The jawless fishes established several key trends in vertebrate design, including the development of the head, an elongate body with clearly defined functional regions, the earliest paired appendages, eyes, and increasingly calcified bony structures on the exterior and interior of the body. The jawless fishes, however, were in some ways the victims of their own success. Their head armor and bony scales made them heavy, clumsy swimmers, destined for bottom feeding. Their basal fins and tails were not designed for swimming in the open ocean and restricted the fishes' habitat to the floors of oceans and freshwater lakes. The jawless feeding orifices of the agnathans also restricted the kinds of food they could consume.

SUMMARY

This chapter described the rise of the jawless fishes from the Late Cambrian Epoch and Ordovician Period to the close of the Devonian Period.

1. The earliest vertebrates are called Agnatha ("no jaw") or jawless fishes; they are a collection of ocean and freshwater vertebrates that predate the development of bony jaws.
2. Jawless fishes range in time from the Early Cambrian to the close of the Devonian Period (525 million to 359 million years ago); they were most widespread during the Silurian and Devonian Periods.
3. Key anatomical traits of agnathans included a simple, round, jawless mouth opening; a cartilaginous skeleton; bony armor plates and scales; a lack of true fins; simple tails; paired eyes; and gill slits or openings on the side of the head.
4. The bilateral symmetry of agnathans resulted in a well-defined body plan based on a sense of direction: Forward and backward motion were relative to the anterior (head) and posterior (tail) ends of the animal.
5. Groups within the Agnatha include the living lampreys and hagfishes and extinct groups that include the Myllokunmingia and Conodonta, the Astraspida and Arandaspida, the Heterostraci, the Anaspida, the Thelodonti, and the Osterostraci, Galeaspida, and Pituriaspida.
6. Heterostraci were one of the most diverse and abundant groups of agnathans, with about 300 species that ranged in time from the Early Silurian to Late Devonian epochs (430 million to 370 million years ago).
7. Osteostracans were possibly the most advanced of the jawless vertebrates and have many affinities with the jawed fishes that followed.
8. Jawless fishes established several key trends in vertebrate design that led to the evolution of the jawed and bony fishes.

6

Vertebrate Innovations

The evolution of early vertebrate anatomy took many small but incrementally significant steps during the time of the jawless fishes. It was during the time of the agnathans that the vertebrate body plan evolved; this involved, most importantly, the formation of the head region, a cartilaginous skeleton, a brain center, eyes, body armor, jawless feeding mechanisms, and the ability to maneuver with some skill in the water. These early fish, although considered predatory, were filter feeders and mostly dwelled on the ocean floor. Filter feeders are limited by the size and kind of food they can take in. This limits their ability to become larger, more dominant creatures.

By the Late Silurian Epoch, about 420 million years ago, another innovation was taking place in the anatomy of the vertebrates. This was the appearance of the first fishes with jaws and a transition from filter feeding to biting food. The development of the first jaws was nothing short of a revolution for backboned creatures. Without jaws, vertebrates may have been relegated to the backwaters of Earth history and may never have left the shallows of the ocean to conquer the land. Other dramatic anatomical innovations also led to the expansion of backboned creatures into many new modes of life.

THE ORIGIN OF JAWS

The first jaws evolved as a modification of the gill arches of the pharynx. Jawless fishes had a simple, round mouth opening and no teeth. The mouth led to a tubular structure flanked on the sides by multiple gill openings, which sometimes numbered as many as 10. The gill openings were in turn supported by a series of jointed,

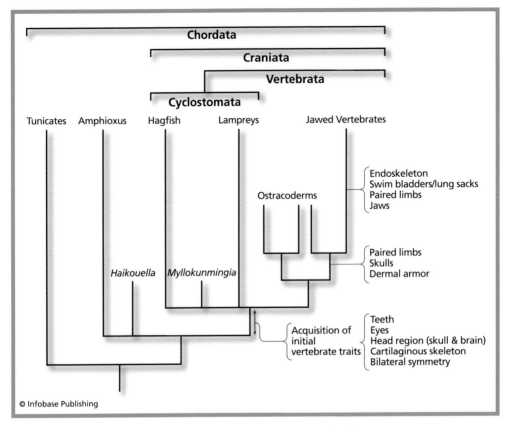

Chordata

Craniata

Vertebrata

Cyclostomata

Tunicates   Amphioxus   Hagfish   Lampreys   Jawed Vertebrates

Endoskeleton
Swim bladders/lung sacks
Paired limbs
Jaws

Ostracoderms

Paired limbs
Skulls
Dermal armor

Haikouella   *Myllokunmingia*

Teeth
Eyes
Acquisition of   Head region (skull & brain)
initial   Cartilaginous skeleton
vertebrate traits   Bilateral symmetry

© Infobase Publishing

The evolution of innovative anatomical traits of early vertebrates

cartilaginous arches just behind the mouth. Muscles contracted and expanded the gill arches to pump water through the gills. The agnathan head region also had a braincase positioned between the frontmost of the gill arches.

As the agnathans advanced, the mouth opening became larger in some taxa, and the anterior gill arches gradually folded over forward at the center joint and became the upper and lower jaws. These were attached by ligaments to the braincase, which anchored them. Pharyngeal muscles that once were used to pump water adapted to power the opening and closing action of the jaws. The first teeth were nothing more than bumps that **derived** from adjacent scales of the agnathan's dermal armor. These scales were composed of dentine, like modern vertebrate teeth, and gradually became larger, sharper, and more specialized over many millions of years of fish evolution.

The Importance of Jaws

The evolution of the first jaws had a profound effect on the direction of vertebrate development. Jaws were the vertebrate's meal ticket away from the life of a bottom-dwelling filter feeder to that of a free-swimming, agile predator. With jaws came the ability to eat larger types of plant and animal food. This opened up entirely new adaptive opportunities that affected the growth, range, and design of fish. Jaws improved the predatory skills of an animal by providing options for capturing, holding, manipulating, and processing food that were never available to agnathans. The ability to increase nutritional intake led to the development of the stomach for storing and digesting food. Vertebrates grew larger, had more food options, and spread into increasingly diverse habitats. Moveable jaws allowed fishes to eat a wider variety and size of invertebrates but also led to a fish-eat-fish world of increasingly specialized jaw mechanisms.

The development of jaws also separated the functions of eating and breathing, which previously had been joined in jawless fishes. During the early evolution of fishes, when these two vital functions were joined, each function was somewhat compromised by having to accommodate the other. When vertebrates divided these functions into two separate anatomical mechanisms, eating and breathing functions began to advance rapidly in tandem. This improved the adaptability of fishes to many environmental conditions. Gills gradually became larger, with more filaments; this improved the fishes' ability to extract oxygen from the water. The size and function of jaws adapted to the habits and food sources available to different taxa of fish, and teeth became increasingly specialized.

(continues on page 104)

THINK ABOUT IT

Living Fishes Without Jaws

Some kinds of fishes still survive without the benefit of jaws. The only living relatives of the extinct agnathans are jawless fishes from two recognized subphyla: the Hyperotreti, or hagfishes, and the Cephalaspidomorphi, or lampreys.

There are about four genera and 20 species of known hagfishes. Hagfishes range in length from about 18 inches (46 cm) to 45 inches (116 cm). Considered the most primitive group of living chordates, the hagfishes are found in cold-water marine environments in both hemispheres. Hagfishes lack paired fins and vertebrae; they rely on a slender notochord for support along the axis of their bodies. Hagfishes are blind but have a strong sense of smell. Long and eel-like, the hagfish has a frill-like fin at the anterior end. The creature's round, open mouth is encircled by four pairs of sensory tentacles. Hagfishes live buried in the bottom sand or mud of their marine environment. They feed on soft-bodied invertebrates but also scavenge dead or dying fish in a most remarkable way. They enter the open mouth

The hagfish is a living jawless fish.

Lampreys use a suckerlike mouth and teeth to attach themselves to the outside of a fish so they can suck the fish's blood.

of a weakened or dead fish and eat the body from the inside out, leaving behind an empty carcass that consists only of skin and bones.

Lampreys are commonly found in temperate waters of lakes and oceans. There are about nine genera and 40 species of living lampreys. The eel-like body of the lamprey can range from 5 to 40 inches (13 to 100 cm) long. The lamprey has a tail fin but lacks paired appendages. Unlike hagfishes, lampreys have eyes. All lampreys breed in freshwater, but some species migrate to the sea at maturity. Lampreys include parasitic and nonparasitic varieties. The lampreys' most notable anatomic features are a round, suckerlike mouth encircled by numerous teeth and a tongue with filelike rasps. Parasitic species of lampreys use their suckerlike mouths and teeth to attach themselves to the outside of a fish and then use their rasping tongues to scrape away the bony scales on the skin of their prey. After it clears a spot with its tongue, a lamprey will puncture the skin of its prey and suck the fish's blood.

The giant placoderm *Dunkleosteus*—the largest predator of the Devonian oceans—attacks the shark *Cladoselache*, which was 6 feet (about 2 m) long.

(continued from page 101)

There was plenty of room for experimentation as well. The largest predator of the Devonian Period was the enormous fish *Dunkleosteus* (see Placoderms below). Growing to lengths of 30 feet

(10 m), *Dunkleosteus* was a somewhat clumsy swimmer. Nevertheless, this monstrous creature was at the top of the food chain. Instead of classic teeth made of dentine, it sported a powerful jaw lined with jagged, axelike bony plates that could slice its prey into bite-size morsels.

All but a few parasitic kinds of jawless fishes—the hagfish and the lampreys—became extinct after the rapid rise of jawed fishes. For the purpose of classification, all jawed fishes are placed within the group *gnathostomes* ("jaw-mouthed"), which includes the early bony fishes and cartilaginous fishes (sharks and ray, for example).

Jaws expanded the predatory opportunities for fishes and led to the refinement of other anatomical features that favored the ability to seek prey and the ability to escape predators. Chief among these features were those that improved swimming ability.

FINS AND TAILS: IMPROVING THE MOBILITY OF EARLY FISHES

What is a fish if not an excellent swimmer? This ability can be assumed in the fishes that live today. The ability to swim with power and maneuverability was not an inherent feature of the earliest vertebrates, however. The ability to swim effectively evolved over time as the first fishes adapted to changing habitats and lifestyles. Jaws were the catalyst that enabled fishes to move up from a bottom-dwelling lifestyle to that of an active swimmer.

Swimming did not come easily to the first vertebrates. The ribbonlike or tubular bodies of the Myllokunmingiida and Conodonta probably could wriggle rapidly but probably did so without much maneuverability. Most other jawless fishes adapted to the lifestyle of bottom-dwelling vacuum cleaners. They sucked up food as they hovered over the ocean floor. Their bodies usually were weighed down by dermal armor and lacked any but the most rudimentary, ribbonlike fin appendages, and their tails were inadequate for the kinds of navigation required by truly agile swimmers. Exceptions to this rule included the osteostracans and some advanced members of the anaspids.

The osteostracans were the first fish to have true paired fins on their sides. Anaspids such as *Rhyncholepis* had a pair of fins positioned closer to the bottom side of the body, just past the head region. Both of these experiments hinted at numerous improvements to fin and tail anatomy that bloomed fully in jawed fishes. Some agnathans also had remarkably streamlined bodies; but no known agnathan exhibited the entire array of adaptations required for highly maneuverable swimming: the fins, tails, and streamlined body that are so familiar in today's fishes. These traits came together for the first time after the appearance of jawed fishes.

The presence of jaws intensified the evolution of fishes in directions that made them more active and mobile. Traits that favored improved maneuverability were paramount in this development and marked yet another significant milestone in the evolution of vertebrates.

The bodies of jawed fishes became increasingly more streamlined than those of their agnathan predecessors. Water is a thick medium, and a creature must have a low-resistance profile to glide through it easily. The streamlining of the fish body began with the anterior or snout end. Jawed fishes did away with the heavy dermal armor plates of the agnathans and developed a narrow, pointed anterior that could slice through the water like a wedge. Just behind the head of a jawed fish is the thickest, largest part of the body. From there the body narrows significantly, further reducing resistance to the water and minimizing turbulence.

Having a streamlined body was a significant improvement for jawed fishes, but their full potential as active, agile swimmers was not completed until they developed a full complement of fins. There are several requirements for becoming an active swimmer in the world of the jawed fishes:

- *Tail (caudal) fin.* This fin has to be large, muscular, and easily flapped from side to side (not up and down) to muscle a fish through the water. A tail is the motor of a fish; it provides nearly endless thrust for moving forward.

- *One or two dorsal (back) fins*. Without a dorsal fin, a fish would roll over when the tail thrust was forward. A dorsal fin is a stabilizer that prevents a fish from rolling over uncontrollably.
- *Ventral (anal) fin*. This fin is positioned on the underside of a fish, near the base of the tail (the location of the anus). Like the keel of a boat, the ventral fin is a stabilizer. It is used for changing direction.
- *Paired pectoral fins (at the shoulder) and pelvic fins (at the hip)*. These two pairs of fins are positioned anywhere from the lower to the middle side of a fish. Working together, paired fins provide the lift necessary to help a fish go up and down, put on the brakes, or even (in some species) move backward. Paired fins are also like rudders; they help a fish make quick turns to the side. The first fishes to master the seas as superb swimmers were the fast-moving ancestors of sharks and bony fishes.

THE SWIM BLADDER

Another vertebrate innovation that contributed to the success of bony fishes was their ability to remain naturally buoyant in the water. By contrast, sharks, whose bodies are made up of cartilage instead of bone, are heavier than water. There is a good reason why sharks developed as hyperactive swimmers: If sharks stop moving, they sink.

Even the earliest bony fishes had developed a unique new feature that added buoyancy to their bodies. These fishes had a pair of air sacks in the lower abdomen that could be filled with air to allow them to sink to a given level in the water. To control the amount of buoyancy, the earliest jawed fishes gulped or expelled air into these sacks by coming to the surface of the water. In later ray-finned fishes, these air sacks evolved into a swim bladder that could exchange gases internally, allowing the fishes to change their buoyancy without having to come to the surface. Without a swim bladder, a bony fish would have to keep on the move at all times, like a shark.

Not all taxa of bony fishes developed swim bladders. The mostly extinct group known as lungfishes developed lungs for breathing air, like land animals, as well as gills for breathing in water.

THE FIRST JAWED FISHES

The first vertebrates with jaws appeared in the Late Ordovician Epoch. Their size, shape, and general anatomy is reminiscent of the jawless fishes that came before them, but they also share some affinities with the more derived bony fishes and sharks that followed.

These basal members of the gnathostomes are divided into two groups, the Acanthodii, or spiny sharks, and the Placodermi. Neither group appears to be ancestral to fishes that followed, and each became extinct by the end of the Devonian Period.

Acanthodians

The first vertebrates to have jaws were the Acanthodii, or acanthodians, also known by the popular name of "spiny sharks" or "spiny skins." Acanthodians were mostly small fish; they measured from 4 to 6 inches (10 to 15 cm) long. Despite their popular name, they were not related to the sharks. The name "spiny shark" refers to the acanthodians' sharklike, streamlined body and their long upturned tail that resembles that of a true shark.

The body of an acanthodian was slender and tall, with one or two dorsal fins, an anal fin, and as many as six pairs of additional fins along the underside. The eyes were large and perched far forward on the head. The jaws were long, but most acanthodians lacked teeth. These fish probably thrived at middle depths, where their large eyes enabled them to see quite well in the dimmer light. Those species that lacked teeth probably gobbled up smaller fish that could be scooped up in pursuit, gnashing them with their bony jaws or swallowing them whole.

The bodies of these small fishes appear to have adapted in ways that provided them with some degree of protection from larger predators. The fin design of acanthodians was an elegant evolutionary experiment. Most of the fins were composed of a sharp spine to which a web of skin was stretched into a triangular shape. With most of the upper and lower surfaces protected by these spines, acanthodians were probably a distasteful surprise to larger fish that tried to eat them. The backward-aiming spines along the bottom of the acanthodian would most certainly have stuck in the gullet of many a predator. At least one species, *Acanthodes*, may have been able to flex the spines upward when attacked, furthering its chances of escaping.

Although the remains of acanthodian endoskeletons are rarely seen, it is presumed that those skeletons were composed of cartilage like those of earlier jawless fishes. The acanthodian body was covered with tightly fitting scales composed of bone and dentine. Behind the jaws on either side of the head were five gill slits. Depending on the species of acanthodian, these slits were protected by one or more bony flaps. Acanthodians were most abundant during the Devonian Period and lived in saltwater and freshwater habitats.

Placoderms

Looking much like their armored jawless predecessors, the placoderms were a diverse collection of armored jawed fishes. The name placoderm, meaning "plated skins," refers to the large, interlocking bony plates that protected the heads of these fishes. The plates were curved and articulated at their joints to provide flexibility, especially where the head shield met the trunk shield. The body

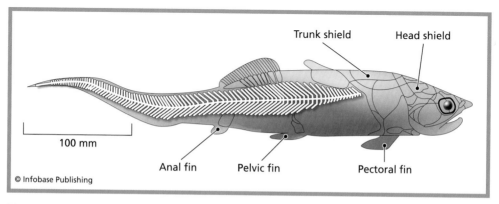

Placoderm anatomy

The arthrodirid placoderm *Groenlandaspis*

behind the trunk region was not armor plated and sometimes had a fine bony mesh protecting it or no scaly covering at all. These common characteristics aside, placoderms came in many sizes, ranging from the diminutive *Groenlandaspis* (19 inches, or 50 cm, long) to the truly monstrous *Dunkleosteus* (30 feet, or 10 m, long), a big-eyed, axe-jawed top predator of the Devonian oceans.

Placoderms arose in the Silurian, were most abundant in the Devonian Period, but died off sharply by the Early Carboniferous. Placoderms consisted of six clades: Acanthothoraci, Rhenanida, Antiarchi, Petalichthyida, Ptyctodontida, and Arthrodira. Four of the most diverse groups were the rhenanids, the antiarchs, the ptyctodontids and the arthrodires.

Rhenanids

The flattened, rounded bodies of the rhenanids disclose a bottom-dwelling life. One of the earliest groups of placoderms, this unusual clade appears superficially very much like the modern rays.

The species *Gemuendina,* from the Devonian of Germany, had pectoral fins that were expanded enormously into winglike lobes. *Gemuendina's* body was flat and rounded, and the creature had a long, narrow tail. The eyes of *Gemuendina* were on the top of its head and were surrounded by armor plates, as were its nostrils and mouth. These armor plates were connected to *Gemuendina's* sides by a matrix of flexible, chain-mail-like dermal armor. Although unrelated to the true rays, which evolved over 250 million years later than *Gemuendina,* the similar body plans of the rhenanids and the rays are a good example of **convergent evolution**.

Model of the rhenanid placoderm *Gemuendina*

Antiarchs

The antiarchs were small. Most reached only about 1 foot (30 cm) in length. They were the most heavily armored of the placoderms, with dermal shields that covered the head and about half the length of the body. Behind the dermal plates, the body was more normally scaled; this made these creatures appear somewhat like normal fishes but with their head in a box. The best known and most widely distributed antiarch species, *Bothriolepis,* is represented by more than 100 specimens from around the world that date from the Late Devonian. *Bothriolepis* had a slender, somewhat flattened body. This indicates that it was a bottom feeder. The creature also had a most unusual pectoral appendage. Just behind the head on either side, *Bothriolepis* had a pair of crablike pectoral fins with tiny spines. *Bothriolepis* presumably used these to help it move about as it hovered on the seafloor or lake bottom.

Ptyctodontids

Ptyctodontids such as *Ctenurella*, from the Late Devonian of Australia, were small fishes about 5 inches (13 cm) long. Ptyctodontids had less armor than any other placoderms. The wide, roundish head of *Ctenurella* featured large eyes close to the dorsal surface. Behind the head, *Ctenurella*'s body tapered quickly to a long, narrow tail with a large dorsal fin. *Ctenurella* also had pairs of sizeable pectoral and pelvic fins, indicating that this small fish probably had above-average maneuverability. Its small but sturdy jaws were equipped with bony tooth surfaces for grinding up shellfish. *Ctenurella* probably roamed over the seafloor, eating tiny urchins and shellfish.

Arthrodires

The most abundant and varied clade of placoderms was the arthrodires, or "jointed neck" fishes. Arthrodires species numbered about 200 and make up about 60 percent of all known placoderms. The diversity of this group is surprising; it is represented by small, armored taxa that measured only 1 foot (30 cm) long and by the largest predator of its time, *Dunkleosteus*, which measured up to 30 feet (10 m). *Coccosteus*, from the Middle and Late Devonian of North America and Europe, was about 16 inches (40 cm) long. It was equipped with light trunk armor, large pectoral and pelvic fins, and a long finned tail. All these features indicate that *Coccosteus* was a good swimmer. Instead of teeth, the arthrodires had sharp, beaklike plates of bone in their jaws that could crunch and slice even the largest prey. A key, unifying trait of arthrodires was an unusual ball and socket joint that articulated the shoulder and head. This allowed an arthrodire to rotate its head backward, giving its formidable mouth an even wider gape.

THE RADIATION OF FISHES

The anatomical innovations of jaws, fins, a streamlined body, and, in some cases, air sacs and swim bladders resulted in the explosive diversity and spread of fishes in the Middle to Late Paleozoic. Among the first experiments in jawed fishes were the acanthodians and placoderms, two groups that exhibit a mosaic of vertebrate experiments in adaptability. The time of the acanthodians and placoderms was short; it extended only from the Late Silurian to the Early Carboniferous. But these creatures represented the first extensive success of jawed vertebrates, and they were followed by the even more successful bony fishes and cartilaginous fishes—Paleozoic lineages with direct ties to fishes living today.

SUMMARY

This chapter explained how jaws evolved in vertebrates and described some other dramatic anatomical innovations that led to the expansion of backboned creatures into many new modes of life.

1. Agnathans, the jawless fishes, established many of the keystones of the vertebrate body plan, including the formation of the head region, the cartilaginous skeleton, the brain center, the eyes, body armor, jawless feeding mechanisms, and the ability to maneuver with some skill in the water.

2. The evolution and diversity of jawless fishes was restricted by their status as filter feeders.

3. The first jaws evolved as a modification of the gill arches of the pharynx.

4. With jaws came the ability to eat larger types of plant and animal food; this opened up entirely new adaptive opportunities that affected the growth, range, and design of fish.

5. Jawed fishes combined several new anatomical features to improve their ability as swimmers; these included tails, fins, streamlined bodies, and air sacks for buoyancy.

6. The anatomical innovations of jaws, fins, a streamlined body, and, in some cases, air sacks and swim bladders resulted in the explosive diversity and spread of fishes in the latter Paleozoic.

7. The first vertebrates to have jaws were the acanthodians, also known by the popular name of "spiny sharks."

7

Cartilaginous Fishes:
The Sharks and Rays

The Chondrichthyes, or "cartilaginous fishes," including sharks, were some of the first vertebrates with jaws and bony teeth. About 60 families of sharks and their kin arose during the Paleozoic Era and became the top ocean predators during the Devonian and Carboniferous Periods.

The Chondrichthyes are so named because all members of this clade have skeletons made of cartilage (gristle), a noncalcified skeletal material. Cartilage is a firm but flexible tissue that does not stretch. Unlike cellular bone, cartilage is not infused with channels for blood vessels or nerves. Cartilage is alive, however, and its cells grow by absorbing oxygen and nutrients from surrounding blood vessels. Cartilage is also present in vertebrates with bony skeletons in the form of connective tissue. Examples of cartilage that can readily be seen in humans include the outer ear flap and the tip of the nose. Cartilage also forms much of the skeleton of vertebrate embryos and young but is calcified into bone over time as the animal matures.

The chondrichthyans are divided into two groups, the Elasmobranchii ("plated gills"), a group that consists of sharks, dogfishes, skates, and rays, and the Holocephali ("whole head"), a group that includes ratfishes and chimaeras. Of these, only the sharks and Holocephali are known from the Paleozoic Era.

TRAITS OF CARTILAGINOUS FISHES

When vertebrates were first evolving, during the Cambrian and Silurian Periods, one trait that led to their great success in the

Paleozoic Era was their ability to swim. The ability to swim effectively involves several interrelated anatomical and physiological specializations. These include having a streamlined body, having a tail and fins for power and maneuverability, and having control over buoyancy in the water. Although the evolutionary link between the earliest cartilaginous fishes and bony fishes is not known, it appears that they were related to a common ancestral line of jawless fishes that seeded their separate lineages with the fundamental characteristics of swimmers. From these jawless vertebrates, the sharks and bony fishes inherited their bilaterally symmetrical body plans and rudimentary fin and tail configurations. Sometime during the Silurian, however, the cartilaginous fishes and bony fishes took separate evolutionary paths. Each developed increasingly efficient improvements on the basal vertebrate body plan for survival in the water.

Even the earliest sharks had a streamlined, elongate shape and a rounded, tapered snout for cutting through the water. The blueprint for shark fins was similar to that for the fins of the first bony fishes, although the construction and size of shark fins differed considerably. All sharks had paired pectoral and pelvic fins. Dorsal fins numbered one or two, and in some species the dorsal fin closest to the head was oversized and reminiscent of the signature dorsal fin seen in modern sharks. The anal fin is not always present in fossil sharks.

The tails of early sharks came in various shapes but most often were **heterocercal**, or asymmetrical with the upper portion being larger than the lower. The heterocercal tail design appears repeatedly in the fossil record of vertebrates; it begins with the jawless fishes and continues in the acanthodians and placoderms, the sharks, and some early ray-finned and lobe-finned fishes. In most cases, including that of the shark, the upper part of the tail is the stiffened end of the bony or cartilaginous vertebral column of the fish. In sharks, the asymmetrical tail fin became a large, powerful source of propulsion.

The task of remaining buoyant in the water is handled differently in sharks than in bony fishes. The shark formula for success in this regard involved two adaptations. First, the cartilaginous skeleton itself is lighter than bone and makes it easier for the shark to remain suspended in the water. A shark, however, is denser than water and would sink if it didn't have another adaptation to help keep it afloat. Sharks do not have swim bladders or lungs like bony fish; they are unable to hold or expel gases to adjust their buoyancy as other fish can. Instead, sharks combine the use of underwater "hydrodynamics" and an oil-saturated liver to control buoyancy.

The pectoral fins of sharks are large and stiff, like the wings of an airplane. The snout is round and tapered and flatter on the underside, similar to the fuselage of an airplane. When a shark swims, the action of water passing across the snout and pectoral fins provides "lift." This is not unlike the aerodynamic principles that enable airplanes to remain aloft in the air. This adaptation alone prevents sharks from sinking, but it requires them to stay in motion. It also prevents them from moving backward.

Another adaptation that enabled the sharks to remain buoyant is a large, oily liver. By accumulating a large amount of low-density oils in the liver, the relative density of a shark in relation to seawater is nearly equalized. This allows the shark to float more easily. A combination of large pectoral fins, large oily livers, and nearly continuous swimming is the shark's solution to buoyancy.

Sharks were some of the first vertebrates to develop teeth. Like their modern descendants, early sharks continually replaced worn or lost teeth. Every tooth that was exposed at the outer edge of the jawline had a "conveyor belt" of new teeth growing behind it. These new teeth cycled into place as each matured. When a new tooth erupted through the jawline, it pushed away the outer tooth in front of it. The teeth were composed of dentine, and they fossilized well. Shed teeth are often the only clues available to early sharks.

Some early sharks exhibited bizarre variations on the tooth-replacement adaptation. One case in point was the Permian shark *Helicoprion*. Instead of having a "conveyor belt" of parallel replacement teeth that grew beneath the surface of the jaw, it had a single circular whorl of teeth positioned at the front of its jaw and a few

Jaws of the great white shark showing replacement teeth in place behind outer teeth

flatter teeth inside its mouth. The spiral of teeth did not shed older teeth but instead continued to grow outwards, adding newer and larger teeth to the outmost surface of the whorl as the shark matured. Specimens of this tooth whorl range in size from 10 to 18 inches (25 to 45 cm) in diameter; they belonged to a sizeable shark that measured up to 20 feet (6 m) long. How did this shark use such an unusual dental battery? Despite the fact that many fossil specimens of the tooth whorl have been found, there is still much debate about how it was affixed to the jaw of *Helicoprion* and how it was used.

One possible scenario for the feeding habits of *Helicoprion* was that it waved its head from side to side to snag soft-bodied squid or mollusks as it swam among them, dragging the invertebrates into its mouth, where the flatter, inside teeth chewed or crushed the prey before the shark swallowed it.

In addition to teeth, sharks also had calcium in their skin in the form of tiny, prickly scales. Like the sharks' teeth, these scales were discarded and replaced on a continual basis. Again like shed teeth, these shed scales provide clues to the presence of ancient sharks despite the fact that their cartilaginous parts were rarely preserved.

Another characteristic of sharks is the presence in males of small, paired appendages on the underside near the anal opening. These are called claspers and are used during reproduction to hold the female tight to the male. The presence of claspers allows paleontologists to distinguish the sex of fossil sharks.

Modern sharks exhibit an extraordinary suite of nerves and senses. They have an excellent sense of smell, and their bodies contain a network of jelly-filled canals called electroreceptors that keep the animals attuned to their environment. One set of receptors can detect the strength and fluctuations of electromagnetic fields, including Earth's magnetic field and fluctuations caused by ocean currents, other animals, and objects in the ocean. Sharks use their ability to sense magnetic fields to steer them on migratory paths.

Additional receptors, located on the top of the head and along the length of the body, can detect vibrations in the water, such as those made by other swimming creatures or injured animals that might become prey. The remains of some fossil sharks provide anatomical evidence that such olfactory and electrosensitive senses were an early part of the evolution of these animals.

THE ORIGIN OF CARTILAGINOUS FISHES

Chondrichthyans were among the first jawed fishes. Until recently, it was thought that these cartilaginous fishes were the last major group of fishes to appear in the fossil record. Evidence for the presence of early sharks, however, is complicated by the fact that there is a natural **bias** against the preservation of cartilage. The best evidence of these fishes' early existence comes from fossilized scales from the Late Ordovician Epoch, 455 million years ago. The earliest records of shark teeth are found in sediments of Early Devonian age, 418 million years ago. This makes the earliest chondrichthyans contemporaries of the armored jawless fishes and the most primitive jawed fishes (acanthodians and placoderms) and predates the rise of bony fishes by about 10 million to 15 million years.

In 2003, a team of Canadian and Australian paleontologists led by Randall Miller of the New Brunswick Museum announced the recovery of the earliest known articulated shark remains. Found in New Brunswick, Canada, and dating from about 409 million years ago, the shark specimen contained a jaw with two rows of teeth lodged in place. It also included one of the oldest known braincases of a chondrichthyan and preserved the presence of paired pectoral fin spines, a feature not previously observed in cartilaginous fishes. The shark measured about 20 to 30 inches (50 to 75 cm) long, about the size of a river salmon. This Canadian specimen predated other previously known fossil sharks by 15 million years.

Even such an important new specimen as this cannot fill many gaps in the evolutionary history of early sharks, however. In some ways, the name of this specimen says it all. Originally described in 1892 on the evidence of a single tooth, it was called *Doliodus problematicus*, "a problematic deceiver." As this name implies, paleontologists have a long way to go before the ancestry of the earliest sharks is better understood.

Most groups of sharks and other cartilaginous fishes of the early Paleozoic bore little resemblance to modern-day forms. It was not until the end of the Paleozoic Era that the line of modern sharks and rays was established, in the group known as the Neoselachii. The Neolselachii were a family of sharks derived from the earlier Elasmobranchii.

SHARKS, RAYS, AND SKATES: THE ELASMOBRANCHS

This group of chondrichthyans is unified by a number of shared characteristics that include paired nasal cavities, three-cusp teeth that are not rooted, five to seven pairs of gills with exposed slits, a heterocercal tail fin, and well-developed senses. The early sharks were otherwise surprisingly diverse in size and design. The largest members of this group became the top predators of the Late Paleozoic oceans. Some species lived in freshwater. Many sharks had unexpectedly bizarre spines, dorsal appendages, and teeth—the source of much puzzlement for paleontologists.

Sharks were the only members of the Elasmobranchii to appear in the Paleozoic Era. The earliest skates, rays, and sawfishes are found in rocks dating from the Late Jurassic Epoch of the Mesozoic Era.

The following are representative sharks from the Paleozoic:

Cladoselache. One of the best known of the early sharks, *Cladoselache* is found in Late Devonian sediments in Ohio. It was from 3.5 to 6 feet (1 to 1.8 m) long and had a rounded, streamlined body reminiscent of modern sharks. *Cladoselache* differed from later sharks in that it lacked an anal fin, had two closely spaced dorsal fins around the midpoint of the back, and had one bladelike spine that projected from the leading edge of each dorsal fin. The tail was heterocercal and strongly forked. *Cladoselache*'s large, paddlelike pectoral fins were stiffened by cartilage. Except for some calcified scales around its large eyes and the margin of the tail, the skin of *Cladoselache* was smooth and uncharacteristic of later sharks, which have sandpaper-like skin on much of their body. *Cladoselache* had five to seven gill slits. Although *Cladoselache* superficially resembled modern sharks, the placement and structure of the paired fins, the smaller size and placement of the dorsal fins, the lack of an anal fin, and a tail that was more evenly forked than that of modern sharks reveal the primitive features of *Cladoselache*.

Denaea. Like *Cladoselache*, this early shark from the Late Devonian had a profile similar to that of modern sharks. It was between 1 and 3.5 feet (0.3 to 1 m) long. Unlike *Cladoselache*, *Denaea* had but one dorsal fin, and that fin did not have an associated bony spine. The pectoral fins of *Denaea* were large and stiff and had a backward-pointing, whiplike extension, the purpose of which is unknown. The pelvic fins were much larger than in *Cladoselache*. The skull was long; the eyes were oversized in comparison with those of later sharks, and the snout protruded to form a distinctive, streamlined anterior point. The tail fin was large, stiff, forked, and heterocercal.

Falcatus. Dating from the Carboniferous, *Falcatus* is known among early sharks for having several unusually exaggerated features. It was a small shark that measured only about 6 inches (15 cm) long. Its heterocercal tail was strongly forked and tall, its paired pectoral and pelvic fins were uncharacteristically small, and the profile of its head was strongly triangular, with a jutting snout. Most curious was an adaptation of the first dorsal fin into a long, protruding shoulder spine that hung over the head like a stanchion for a street light. This fin and the top of the creature's head were covered with small, denticlelike scales. Many specimens of this shark have been found in Montana, and it is clear from the fossil record that females (lacking claspers) did not have this unusual dorsal fin. The dorsal fin was probably for display purposes in courting a mate.

Stethacanthus and *Akmonistion*. These sharks from the Late Devonian to Late Carboniferous have been found in Scotland, Illinois, Iowa, Montana, and Ohio. *Stethacanthus* and *Akmonistion* were small; they ranged from about 10 inches to 4 feet (254 cm to 1.2 m) long. Both animals were adorned with a unique outgrowth of the dorsal fin, the shape of which has been described as that of a large, rounded shaving brush mounted on an anvil. The upper surface was covered with toothlike denticles as was a matching patch on the animal's brow. The base of this appendage was embedded just above the shoulder area and was composed of calcified cartilage strands. The foot of the base was connected to a hard spine made of dentine. Only male specimens had this extravagant dorsal appendage, suggesting that it was related to courtship and sexual display.

Helicoprion. Found in Early Permian deposits in Russia, North America, Japan, and Australia, *Helicoprion* was part of a radiation

The shark *Helicoprion* had a disc-like whorl of teeth affixed to its lower jaw.

of Late Paleozoic sharks with unusual dental batteries. Its adaptation for tooth replacement included a spiral-shaped tooth assembly fitted between the two lower jaws. Unlike other families of sharks that shed older teeth, *Helicoprion* and its kin retained their older, smaller teeth as a part of the tooth whorl. The tooth whorl ranged in size from about the diameter of a dinner plate in average-sized specimens to as large as three feet (1 m) in diameter in the largest known examples. These teeth of *Helicoprion* probably worked in conjunction with a flat, bony grinding surface in the upper jaw. How this shark used the tooth whorl is not entirely understood. One view is that *Helicoprion* swung its head back and forth to hook passing soft-bodied squid and other invertebrates in its path. Once in the mouth, the prey could have been crushed and chewed between the tooth whorl and the grinding surface in the upper jaw.

The shark *Edestus* had unusual dentition, which consisted of two jaw bones that protruded straight out of its mouth.

Edestus. Another puzzling shark is *Edestus*, from the Carboniferous of the United States. *Edestus* was a large shark; it measured about 20 feet (6 m) long. This great size made it one of the largest predators of its time. *Edestus*'s unusual dentition consisted of two tooth-bearing elements that protruded straight out of the shark's mouth at the symphysis, in front of its face. Each element had up to 10 teeth lined up in a row along the jawline. This spectacular jaw could have been used to snap at prey or perhaps snag them with glancing blows as this large shark swam through their midst.

Belantsea. Dating from the Early Carboniferous Epoch of Montana, *Belantsea* was a member of a specialized group of cartilaginous fishes that were unlike the traditional image of a shark.

(continues on page 126)

THINK ABOUT IT

Andrzej P. Karpinsky and the Puzzle of the Tooth Whorl

Paleozoic fossil fishes are rarely found fully inscribed in rocks, yet even the most fragmentary specimen often yields obvious clues to the nature of the creature that left it behind. Fish scales, tails, fins, skulls, and vertebrae, even when found in isolation from other skeletal parts, can still reveal much about the size, anatomy, and lifestyle of the associated fish. Every once in a while, however, a fossil appears that tests the know-how of even the most meticulous and imaginative paleontologist. Such was the case of *Helicoprion*, a fossil shark from the Early Permian.

The first described specimen of *Helicoprion* was discovered in the Ural Mountains of Russia in 1898 and described in 1899 by paleontologist Andrzej P. Karpinsky (1847–1936), the director of the Imperial Russian Geological Survey. The specimen consisted of a single, spiral-like structure that, on closer inspection, proved to be a whorl of sharklike teeth. There were 156 teeth in the whorl, which measured about 10 inches (24 cm) in diameter. The teeth were largest on the outside of the spiral and diminished in size toward the center of the spiral. Unlike the teeth of other sharks, these teeth were not shed and appeared to be permanently embedded in a spiraling ribbon of bone. Despite having nothing but the tooth whorl to go by, Karpinsky immersed himself in the task of deciphering the mystery of this fossil. He named the shark *Helicoprion*, meaning "spiral saw," and wrote a 110-page paper describing the historical, geological, chemical, histological, and biological aspects of this fossil and its relationship to other sharks. The only things he was at a loss to explain were how the teeth had been attached to the shark and how the shark had used them. Karpinsky offered some ideas in the form of sketches that variously placed the tooth whorl in such unlikely places as the tail, the lower jaw, and as an upward spiraling extension of the upper jaw, like the nose of an elephant.

Karpinsky was a respected scientist, yet his fellow researchers could not resist jumping into the *Helicoprion* guessing game. In 1900,

Karpinsky and others suggested many unusual solutions to the tooth whorl mystery.

the American Edwin T. Newton favored a dorsal fin location for the whorl, making it a means of defense. The debate continued long after Karpinsky's death in 1936. In 1952, Russian paleontologist Dimitri Ob-ruchev suggested that the tooth whorl would have been an obstruction in the lower jaw; he favored a location in the upper jaw, where it could have served as a defense mechanism. In 1962, another American, Theo-dore H. Eaton Jr., suggested that both the upper and lower jaws were equipped with a tooth whorl.

By the 1990s, many specimens of the *Helicoprion* tooth whorl had been discovered in widely dispersed Permian deposits in Russia, Spitsbergen,

(continues)

(continued)

Japan, Australia, the Canadian Arctic, British Columbia, Idaho, California, and Nevada. The largest specimens measure more than three feet (1 m) in diameter, suggesting that they belonged to a large shark that may have measured as long as 20 feet (6 m).

Although significant remains of the rest of the body of *Helicoprion* are yet to be discovered, the Danish paleontologist Svend E. Bendix-Almgreen recovered fragments of the skull along with a tooth whorl in 1966. These fragments—the best clues that we have to the position and utility of the mysterious spiral saw—place the tooth whorl at the front of the bottom jaw. Unlike Karpinsky, who imagined an elephantlike, scrolling jaw, Bendix-Almgreen pictured the tooth whorl as a kind of buzz saw fixed within the mouth and used to snag soft-bodied prey suspended in the water. The upper jaw appears to have been equipped only with a grinding tooth surface against which the tooth whorl could pulverize whatever food it had snagged.

(continued from page 123)

Belantsea had a tall and bulbous body with a short head and large eyes. The fish was not a rapid swimmer; instead, it was adapted to eating hard-bodied shelled creatures that it might find on the seafloor or on reefs. *Belantsea* measured about 3.5 feet (1 m) long. It had armor plating around its mouth and a small number of broad, flattened teeth in its upper and lower jaws. These teeth acted as grinding surfaces on which to crunch hard food such as mollusks. *Belantsea*'s fins were frill-like or petal-like, and the tail was greatly reduced. *Belantsea* was probably most comfortable hovering over the seabed as it picked up shelled creatures with its jaws.

Hybodus. Hybodus first arose during the Carboniferous Period. It and its kin continued to diversify and spread well into the Mesozoic

Belantsea was a tall and bulbous shark with a short head and large eyes.

oceans, where hybodont-related sharks were among the most plentiful and dominant predators in areas now in North America and Europe. Descendants of the hybodonts were still in existence during the Late Cretaceous Epoch and lived alongside modern sharks. *Hybodus* itself had a long body with an unevenly forked, heterocercal tail and relatively small fins. The front of each dorsal fin was composed of a long, sharp spine. *Hybodus* was about 6.5 feet (2 m) long and had two types of teeth: pointed, conical teeth in the front of its jaw and blunt, grinding teeth in the back. The arrangement of the teeth suggests that *Hybodus* would snag prey with its front teeth and then chew it inside the mouth with the blunt teeth. These teeth allowed this shark to have a varied diet that consisted of fish, crustaceans, and bottom-dwelling shelled creatures. Some species of *Hybodus* have been found in freshwater deposits.

Xenacanthus. This eel-like shark dates from the Early Permian of Europe. It was one of the only Paleozoic sharks that lived exclusively

Model of the Carboniferous shark *Hybodus*. It had two types of teeth: pointed, conical teeth in the front of its jaw and blunt, grinding teeth in the back.

in freshwater habitats. The shark is named *Xenacanthus* after the "strange spine" attached to the top of its head—a spine that looks like an automobile antenna. *Xenacanthus* was generally a small fish, about 2.5 feet (75 cm) long, but some of its kin reached lengths of 7 feet (2.1 m). Its body was elongate and tapered back to the tip of its tail. It had a long, single dorsal fin fashioned as a frill along the entire length of the back. *Xenacanthus* probably wriggled its body back and forth to propel itself forward. Each of *Xenacanthus*'s teeth had a crown consisting of two sharp, conical points. The upper and lower jaws were lined with these small teeth and must have allowed *Xenacanthus* to bite down with a firm grip on its wriggling freshwater prey. The paired fins of this shark were small. The long and low profile of *Xenacanthus* was well adapted for slinking through overgrown lake and rivers, not unlike a large newt.

The eel-like shark *Xenacanthus* dates from the Early Permian of Europe.

CHIMAERAS AND OTHER HOLOCEPHALIANS

The Holocephali is a subclass of cartilaginous fishes that first appeared in the Late Devonian. The only surviving descendants of the holocephalians are the chimaeras or ratfishes. Extinct forms include members of two known groups, the Iniopterygiformes and Chondrenchelyiformes. All date from the Late Devonian and spread during the Carboniferous. It is assumed that most lived in deep waters, like their remaining descendants.

The bizarre-looking holocephalians developed several different body plans but shared the following characteristics: gill slits covered by a single, protective bony plate; lack of scales or body armor; large eyes for seeing at great depths; pelvic claspers used by males to hold females during mating; and an upper jaw that was fused to the cranium coupled with upper and lower broad, fused, dental pavements instead of individual teeth. The biting surface was ideal for crushing the hard parts of shelled creatures. In addition, unlike in elasmobranch sharks, the cartilage forming the upper jaw of holocephalians was fused to the braincase, locking the upper jaw in place without the ability to flex or protrude. This adaptation reinforced the jaws and assisted holocephalians in crunching down on their hard-bodied prey. The structure of the skull was also the source of the name Holocephali, which is Greek for "whole head."

Sibyrhynchus. This taxon and other examples of iniopterygians (a name meaning "neck fin") date from the Late Carboniferous of the United States. These most unusual-looking creatures resembled bug-eyed underwater bats, with fins like flying fish and spines jutting out from the pectoral region just behind the gills. *Sibyrhynchus* and other iniopterygians were small, about 18 inches (45 cm) long. *Sibyrhynchus's* tail was rounded, and the front of the winglike pectoral fins were studded with toothlike denticles.

Iniopteryx. Found in Late Carboniferous deposits of Indiana and Nebraska, *Iniopteryx,* like *Sibyrhynchus,* was an iniopterygian with a suite of oddball anatomical features. From a top down view, *Iniopteryx* resembled a wide-bodied airplane. Its pectoral fins were disproportionately long and flexible. Inside the pectoral fins was a supporting structure of fine cartilaginous rays. The anterior edges of these underwater wings were arrayed with several rows of small, pointed denticles. *Iniopteryx* usually measured less than 12 inches (30 cm) long. There is speculation that *Iniopteryx* and its iniopterygian kin may have been able to glide briefly above the water like modern-day flying fish, to which the iniopterygians are no relation.

Helodus. This member of the Chondrenchelyiformes, or extinct chimaerans, dates from the Carboniferous Period and is found in freshwater sediments in Europe. *Helodus* is something of a mosaic of antique shark features: It had the fins, head, and jaws of a chimaeran but the small teeth and heterocercal tail of other cartilaginous fish. *Helodus* had a more general sharklike profile than did

Iniopterygians ("neck fin") date from the Late Devonian and had a bizarre suite of anatomical shapes and features underscored by a pair of long pectoral fins positioned high on the neck.

later chimaerans from the Mesozoic Era, which more closely resemble modern-day forms of sharks. *Helodus* measured about 1.5 feet (45 cm) long. Like other chondrenchelyiforms, it had moderately large pectoral fins that were placed more toward the lower side of the animal. This is unlike the iniopterygians, the pectorals of which were oversized and placed higher up on the side of the body.

Deltoptychius. This Carboniferous chondrenchelyiform from Ireland and Scotland had the more ratfishlike features associated with later chimaerans from the Mesozoic. These included large eyes, pointed tails, a small skull with a pointed snout, large pectoral fins, and a set of tooth plates, rather than individual teeth, for grinding hard food. Measuring about 18 inches (45 cm) long, *Deltoptychius* was probably a dweller of the seafloor, where its large eyes could help it see in the dim light. It had a large dorsal fin with a tall spine at its base, which suggests that this early line of chimaerans may have been equipped with a poison-tipped spike like some extant species.

LIVING IN THE PAST

Sharks and other cartilaginous fishes have a history going back to the Late Ordovician Epoch, more than 443 million years ago. Although early cartilaginous fishes from the Paleozoic differed significantly from extant species, members of the two main branches of the chondrichthyans—the Elasmobranchii and the Holocephali—survive to this day.

If longevity is a measure of success in the fossil record, sharks and their kin must rank as some of the most successful lines of organisms in the history of the planet. Yet the history of sharks in particular is not one of continual domination of the seas.

The first great radiation of sharks occurred during the Paleozoic Era and peaked during the Devonian, when sharks were the top predators of the sea. Their numbers declined toward the end of the Paleozoic, supplanted first, it seems, by the rapid spread and diversification of bony fishes that continued into the Mesozoic Era. The Mesozoic was the age of reptiles: Dinosaurs ruled the land, and marine reptiles such as the plesiosaurs, mosasaurs, and dophinlike ichthyosaurs spread throughout the seas in large numbers. Modern sharks, the neoselachians, first appeared in the latest part of the Paleozoic, but their numbers were relatively low for another 75 million years. Their multiplication was perhaps constrained by their having to share an overly competitive ocean with large numbers of marine reptiles and bony fishes.

During the Jurassic and Cretaceous Periods, however, sharks diversified once again. They grew in numbers and kinds and reestablished themselves as predators of note in the prehistoric seas. One reason for their resurgence was suggested by paleontologists Detlev Thies and Wolf-Ernst Reif in 1985. In Thies and Reif's scenario, the revitalized diversification of sharks in the Jurassic Period was an opportunistic response to the availability of increasingly abundant food in the form of bony fishes. Sharks of all kinds became more numerous and occupied many different kinds of habitats, including lagoonal, intercoastal, and open ocean environments. This radiation was so successful that sharks exhibiting the characteristics of modern faunas were firmly established by the Early Cretaceous Epoch.

The other important groups of fishes that rose to fill the Paleozoic seas were the Osteichthyans, or bony fishes. The bony fishes eventually became the most plentiful vertebrates of all.

SUMMARY

This chapter traced the Paleozoic evolution of sharks and their kin.

1. The Chondrichthyes, or "cartilaginous fishes," including sharks, were some of the first vertebrates with jaws and bony teeth.

2. The chondrichthyans are divided into two groups, the Elasmobranchii ("plated gills"), consisting of sharks, dogfishes, skates, and rays, and the Holocephali ("whole head").

3. Even the earliest sharks had the blueprint for shark anatomy. This included a streamlined, elongate shape with a rounded, a tapered snout for cutting through the water and fins that were similar in configuration to those of the first bony fishes, although the construction and size of shark fins differed considerably.

4. Sharks have self-replacing teeth; some early taxa, such as *Helicoprion*, developed uniquely complex adaptations for this replacement, including spiral-like tooth whorls.

5. The best evidence of the earliest sharks comes from fossilized scales from the Late Ordovician Epoch, 455 million years ago.

6. The earliest articulated shark remains are from New Brunswick, Canada, from about 409 million years ago.

7. Sharks were the only members of the Elasmobranchii to appear in the Paleozoic Era. The earliest skates, rays, and

sawfishes are found in rocks that date from the Late Jurassic Epoch of the Mesozoic Era.

8. The only surviving descendants of the holocephalians are the chimaeras or ratfishes. Extinct forms include members of two known groups, the Iniopterygiformes and Chondrenchelyiformes. All date from the Late Devonian and spread during the Carboniferous Period.

9. Modern sharks, the neoselachians, first appeared in the Late Paleozoic but did not gain a dominant position as ocean predators until the Jurassic and Cretaceous Periods.

8

BONY FISHES

The most numerous members of the jawed vertebrates are the *Osteichythes*, or bony fishes. This is the last major group of fishes to appear in the fossil record and accounts for more than half of the living groups of vertebrates on land or sea. The osteichthyans date from the Late Silurian. They arose during the heyday of the acanthodians and placoderms but by the Carboniferous Period supplanted them as one of two groups of dominant marine vertebrates. The other new dominant group was that of the cartilaginous sharks and rays. This chapter describes the anatomical characteristics of the bony fishes and introduces prominent groups of these fishes that thrived during the Paleozoic Period.

TRAITS OF BONY FISHES

As their name implies, the osteichthyans were the first fishes with an endoskeleton composed of apatite bone instead of cartilage. Their scales were also composed of bony material such as dentine and enamel. The bony fishes are divided into two clades based on the design of their fin structure. The *Actinopterygii*, or "ray fins," have fins supported by a fanlike bony or cartilaginous architecture. The Sarcopterygii, or "lobe fins," have fleshy fins composed of a core of articulated bones to which muscles and smaller, radiating bones are affixed.

Unlike the successful ray-finned fishes, the lobe-fins are nearly extinct. Less than a dozen species of lobe-finned fishes, mostly lungfishes, are still alive today. Among these extant lobe-finned fishes, however, is the fascinating *Coelacanth*, a living fossil that has remained virtually unchanged since Paleozoic times—an evolutionary

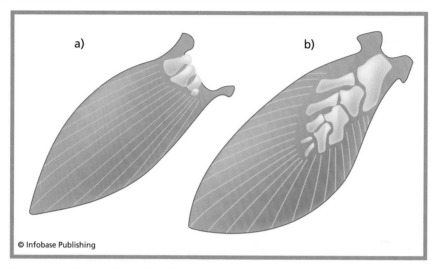

© Infobase Publishing

Two types of early bony fish fins: (a) ray-finned with bony rays leading out from a bony base; and (b) fleshy or lobe fins in which bony rays emanate from bones running along the axis of the fin.

success story if there ever was one. The importance of the lobe-finned fishes to the evolution of terrestrial vertebrates is also significant because it was the lobe-finned fishes' lineage that gave rise to the first limbed animals—the **tetrapods**.

In addition to having a bony endoskeleton and scales, all bony fishes share several other anatomical features. The skull is well formed and heavily armored. Even the gills are protected by a bony flap, unlike the exposed gill slits of the sharks. The teeth are fixed solidly to the jawbones and become increasingly well developed and sharp when compared to those of the acanthodians and placoderms. Early bony fishes also had a pair of air sacks in the lower abdomen that were used to control the fishes' buoyancy.

THE ORIGIN OF BONY FISHES

The appearance of fishes with bony endoskeletons occurred quite suddenly in the fossil record, at least by geologic standards. Bone had appeared earlier, in the agnathans, as an outer covering of the cartilaginous skull and back. At about the same time, in the Early

Devonian Epoch, actinopterygian fishes with completely bony skeletons first appeared. Only recently has fossil evidence emerged for an evolutionary stage that bridges the gap from the cartilaginous jawless fishes to the bony fishes.

What is arguably the earliest known bony fish comes from Late Silurian and Early Devonian strata (410 million to 400 million years ago) of China and Vietnam. This fish, *Psarolepis*, is known from several partial specimens and was at first thought to be a basal member of the lobe-finned fishes. Additional specimens studied by Chinese paleontologist Min Zhu and his colleagues in 1999 suggested that *Psarolepis* was a basal ancestor to both the ray-finned fishes and lobe-finned fishes. The head elements of the fish are the best preserved parts of the available specimens and show a combination of actinopterygian and sarcopterygian features. These features include teeth like those of the lobe-finned fishes and cheekbones like those of the ray-finned fishes. Curiously, *Psarolepis* also had some affinities with basal jawed fishes such as placoderms, including paired fins and large dorsal and pectoral spines unlike any that have been seen in ray-finned or lobe-finned fishes. This remarkable convergence of features associated with jawless as well as jawed fishes makes *Psarolepis* one of the best candidates for a line of primitive bony fishes that was ancestral to bony fishes that followed.

The discovery in Australia in 2001 of a 400 million-year-old fossilized braincase from a fish named *Onychodus* reinforced the idea that the ancestors of bony fishes may have combined features of early sarcopterygians and actinopterygians with primitive features previously restricted to nonbony fishes. This suggests that the evolution of early bony fishes may have involved many parallel developments in ray-finned and lobe-finned fishes.

RAY-FINNED FISHES

There are more than 25,000 living species of ray-finned fishes. They are found in freshwater and saltwater habitats. Their origins in the Paleozoic were marked by rapid diversification until, by the Triassic

Period, they were already the most abundant vertebrate of the seas. This success came at the expense of other, lesser sophisticated fishes, particularly the lobe-finned fishes. The lobe-fins gradually dwindled in numbers during the Mesozoic Era as the ray-finned fishes spread.

Classifying the early ray-finned fishes of the Paleozoic has been a challenge for scientists because these fishes' roots are not entirely understood. As a result, many varied species of early actinopterygians were at one time collectively grouped within the palaeoniscids ("ancient swimmer"), a catch-all category that was **paraphyletic**—a word used to describe a group of organisms that evolved from a common ancestor but that does not include all the descendants of that ancestor.

Another approach to classifying early ray-finned fishes is to assign them to related groups according to the sequence of their appearance in the fossil record. Using this method, three successive radiations of fishes are recognized:

Basal Actinopterygians. This radiation spans the time from the Carboniferous Period to the Triassic Period. It includes the Paleozoic bony fishes discussed in *The First Vertebrates*. This group is synonymous with fossil fishes once grouped as the chondrosteans.

Neopterygians. This radiation spans the time from the Triassic Period to the Jurassic Period and has its roots in the Late Permian. The neopterygian ("new fins") radiation includes fishes once grouped within the paraphyletic category of holosteans. This means, therefore, that this radiation includes some but not all descendants of an inferred common ancestor, which does not provide a firm basis for classification.

Teleosts. This radiation spans the time from the Jurassic Period to the present. The teleosts are the most abundant fish species living today; nearly all modern fishes are teleosts.

Traits of Ray-Finned Fishes

The early actinopterygians of the Paleozoic were generally small. Although some taxa were larger, most ranged in size from 2 to

8 inches (5 to 20 cm) long. They had short snouts and the large eyes characteristic of active predators. Unlike the thick and stiffened fins found in sharks, the fins of the actinopterygians were flexible, lightweight, and thin. This gave these fishes increased maneuverability.

The ray-finned fishes adopted the successful arrangement of fins seen in the acanthodians and placoderms and that is still seen in most modern fishes. They had pairs of pectoral and pelvic fins, one or two dorsal fins, and an anal fin on the ventral side, just before the tail. The tail, although found in various shapes, was strongly forked and arranged in a vertical configuration. It was flapped from side to side to power the fish. The way the tail was forked is a differentiation trait between the early actinopterygians and later fishes. The top fork was a bony spine to which a fin membrane was attached to form the lower fork. The lower part of the fork was a lightweight fin reinforced with bony rods. It reminds one of a sail attached to a mast.

The thick, armored scales of basal ray finned-fishes were composed of several bony layers, including dentine topped with a shiny enamel. In some species, such as *Cheirolepis* and *Moythomasia,* the scales overlapped and were locked together by a peg and socket design for articulation as the animal flexed. The scales were arranged in long, vertically oriented or diagonal rows. Despite the armored natures of the scales, the dermal covering was light enough not to impede these rapidly swimming predators.

The jaws of Paleozoic ray-finned fishes underwent two distinct evolutionary phases. The earliest actinopterygians had small but strong jaws for snapping at prey. The top jaw was fixed to the skull, and the lower jaw was hinged to open and shut against the upper jaw. This gave the fish a kind of long, grinning jaw that operated like the jaw of a ventriloquist's dummy. These fishes relied on powerful jaw muscles and a quick snap of the lower jaw to snag their prey.

By the Late Permian Epoch, with the rise of the neopterygians, the jaws of the ray-finned fishes took a dramatic turn. The top jaw was no longer fixed in place but had a loose-fitting hinge. As the bottom jaw opened, the top jaw drew downward and forward. This gave the fish a rounder mouth and a sucking action to draw the prey into the mouth cavity before the fish bit it. The loosened connections of the jaw also encouraged the evolution of stronger muscles; this gave the neopterygians a potentially stronger bite. Other improvements seen in neopterygians included lighter scales and increasingly powerful and streamlined fins and tails.

The body plans of different families of actinopterygians varied widely and are best discussed while discussing representative species.

Basal Actinopterygians

Early actinopterygians had limited range in the oceans of the Late Paleozoic; they were outnumbered by lobe-finned fishes and later by more advanced ray-finned fishes, beginning with the neopterygians. The early actinopterygians were, however, the most diverse freshwater fishes of that time.

The only living relatives of the basal actinopterygians are the heavily armored bichirs, found in equatorial Africa; the long-bodied sturgeons, known as a source of caviar and found in freshwater river systems, lakes, and coastal waters of Asia, Russia, Central Asia, Europe, and North America; and paddlefishes, large, freshwater fishes that have a large mouth and a peculiar paddle-shaped snout and that are found in the southern United States.

Following is a guide to some of the best known species of basal actinopterygians of the Paleozoic Era.

Cheirolepis. *Cheirolepis,* found in Middle Devonian rocks of what today is Scotland, was an early form of ray-finned fish. Its body was long and thin and measured up to 22 inches (55 cm) long. *Cheirolepis* was equipped with a strong tail and large pectoral and pelvic fins; this design made it a fine swimmer. The downward-turning tail had a sharp row of scales on its dorsal edge to help the fish cut through the water more quickly. *Cheirolepis's* scales were small and rectangular and were arranged in diagonal rows. The skull of *Cheirolepis* was boxy and composed of moveable parts; this allowed the skull to expand dynamically as the gape of the mouth widened to take in prey. *Cheirolepis* probably could swallow other fishes up to about two-thirds its own size. *Cheirolepis* had many short but sharp teeth that lined three distinct bones around the edge of the mouth: the maxilla and premaxilla on the upper skull edge and the dentary of the lower jaw. This arrangement of tooth-bearing jawbones is a feature seen in most later vertebrates.

Mimia. This fish, from the Late Devonian of Australia, is similar to *Cheirolepis* but slightly more derived in its features. Like *Cheirolepis*, it was a good swimmer; but *Mimia's* tail was more forked, its dorsal and anal fins were larger and more triangular in shape, and the profile of the body was taller and more streamlined that that of *Cheirolepis*. In addition to having teeth in the maxilla, premaxilla, and dentary bones, Mimia also had teeth along the midline of the roof of the mouth.

Moythomasia. This basal actinopterygian is found in Middle to Late Devonian strata of Australia and North America. Like *Cheirolepis*, *Moythomasia* had an unusual coat of interlocking scales that could bend and flex as the fish moved; this made it an agile swimmer. This small fish measured about 3.5 inches (9 cm) long, had the large eyes characteristic of these early ray-finned fishes, and had a downward-turning tail capped by a row of backward-aiming bony nodes along its dorsal edge.

Canobius. *Canobius* is from the Early Carboniferous of Scotland and measures a small 3 inches (7 cm) long. It had a body plan similar to that of *Moythomasia*, only smaller. It had a deeper, rounder body, a downturned tail, and large pectoral and anal fins. Its head was small and tapered, with extraordinarily large eyes for the size of the skull. Inside its mouth was an experiment in jaw design. In other fishes, the upper jawbones were attached at a slight angle to the bony braincase above, bowing the jaws outward toward the cheeks. In *Canobius*, the jawbones were attached perpendicularly,

Canobius was a tiny ray-finned fish from Scotland.

suspended vertically inside the mouth. This allowed for a little more room in the cheeks, enabled the fish to open its mouth wider, and allowed it to pass more water over the gills. The gills of *Canobius* became greatly enlarged over those of other early ray-finned fishes. The experimental jaw arrangement not only improved the respiration and activity level of this little fish, but also allowed it to suck in more food from the surrounding water.

Amphicentrum. First described in the 1860s, this species was found in Carboniferous deposits of England. *Amphicentrum* was about 7 inches (18 cm) long and had an unusually deep, disc-shaped and flattened body, with a rudimentary forked tail that consisted of an upper bony spine from which a more delicate fin flap was dropped. In general appearance, *Amphicentrum* is reminiscent of modern reef fishes such as angelfish. Its paired fins were greatly reduced and the dorsal and anal fins modified into long, ribbonlike strips. Its teeth were blunted rather than pointed, which suggests that *Amphicentrum* may have eaten food that required crushing, such as small, shelled invertebrates or armored fish.

Guildayichthys. First described in 2000, this early ray-finned fish dates from the Early Carboniferous of Montana. It shares some

Model of the early actinopterygian *Palaeoniscum*

general affinities with *Amphicentrum,* from England. Like *Amphicentrum, Guildayichthys* has a round, disclike shape to its body. The specimens of *Guildayichthys* are tiny; some measure only about 2 inches (5.4 cm) long. *Guildayichthys* was a marine species rather than a freshwater fish. Other distinguishing features include a tail that is only minimally forked and robust pectoral, dorsal, and anal fins that were most certainly capable of helping this small fish to maneuver quickly. *Guildayichthys*'s mouth was lined with short, conical teeth, which made it a plucking and grazing feeder.

Palaeoniscum. One of the last of the "early" line of actinopterygians, *Palaeoniscum* had a long, streamlined body shaped like a projectile. Measuring up to 12 inches (30 cm) long, this fish was powered by a large, deeply forked tail and guided by sharp, triangular shaped dorsal, anal, and paired fins. Its mouth was long and lined with tiny, sharp teeth. *Palaeoniscum* lived in freshwater environments of England, Germany, Greenland, and the United States, where it was one of the most successful radiations of the basal acti-nopterygians that dominated inland lakes and streams of the world toward the end of the Paleozoic.

Neopterygians

Following the radiation of basal actinopterygians, a new lineage of ray-finned fishes arose in the Late Permian Epoch and became prominent in the Mesozoic and Cenozoic Eras. Neopterygians represent a second major wave in the evolution of ray-finned fishes. Occupying both freshwater and marine environments, neopterygians were distinguished from early ray-finned fishes by major changes to the jaws, the shape of the skull, and the tail. In neopterygians, the tooth-bearing maxilla and dentary bones jutted forward from the face and were usually lined with sharp, pointed teeth. The neopterygian mouth had a wider, gaping orifice which, when opened, caused the cheeks to expand sideways, sucking in more water. The tail was no longer supported by a dorsal bony spine but had a more evenly forked design supported by a lightweight fan of bony rods.

The neopterygians include four main groups of fishes. The semionotids were early neopterygians, now extinct. The lepisosteids include the living species and first appeared in the Cretaceous Period. The bowfins, or halecomorphids, arose in the Triassic Period and have a surviving member that lives in freshwaters of North America. Most significantly, the group of the neopterygia is also the stem group from which modern fish, the Teleostei, arose. The teleosts include most of the bony fish familiar to us today.

The semionotids appeared in the Permian Period. The other clades of neopterygians evolved after the Paleozoic. *Semionotus* is the best known member of the semionotids. Members of this taxon were small, streamlined swimmers that lived in freshwater and marine habitats. *Semionotus* was about 5 inches (13 cm) long. It had the jutting lower jaw of other neopterygians, but instead of sharp

Fossil of the neopterygians *Semionotus*

teeth, *Semionotus* had peglike teeth. The jaws were relatively short compared to the jaws of other neopterygians but projected forward from the snout. The fish's tail was forked and fanned with delicate bony rods. On the midline of the back, between the neck and the dorsal fin, *Semionotus* had a series of bony spines that enabled the fish to cut through the water more effectively. *Semionotus*'s dorsal fin was almost square and pointed backward; the anal fin was long and pointed downward. Based on the many numbers of specimens found in some locations, it appears that *Semionotus* traveled in schools of its own kind.

LOBE-FINNED FISHES

Lobe-finned fishes—the sarcopterygians—arose during the Early Devonian Epoch and were one of the first successful groups of bony fishes. Their numbers dwindled by the end of the Paleozoic, with the rise of the ray-finned fishes, but not before some members of the sarcopterygian group successfully evolved to become the first terrestrial vertebrates. There are still many questions about which of the lobe-finned fishes were most closely related to land animals.

For the purpose of this discussion, lobe-finned fishes will be placed into the following categories:

- *Porolepiformes*: an early group of sarcopterygians, now extinct.
- *Osteolepiformes*: an early group of sarcopterygians, now extinct, with ancestral roots to land animals.
- *Actinistia*: the coelacanths, the only marine form of lobe-finned fishes that survives to this day.
- *Dipnoi*: the lungfishes, which are still represented by three living freshwater species.

Traits of Lobe-Finned Fishes

The sarcopterygians were generally larger than their ray-finned relatives. They ranged, on average, from 10 to 40 inches (25 to 100 cm) long with some much larger members. Some, but not all, members of the group were largely marine creatures, which is probably one reason why the smaller ray-finned fishes found more success in freshwater habitats during the Paleozoic Era. Body shape was generally long, narrow and rounded. A key distinguishing feature of all lobe-finned fishes is the placement and structure of their fins.

Unlike the lightweight, fanned fins of ray-finned fishes, the fins of lobe-finned fishes were distinctively muscular and hefty. Each fin was built around an articulated core of thick bone reinforced with muscle and radiated a skin-covered fringe of delicate rays. The pectoral fins were the strongest of the set; this eventually led to their adaptation as **forelimbs** for the terrestrial-bound members of the lobe-finned clan.

The tails of the lobe-finned fishes varied widely from group to group. Some showed affinities with the sharply forked tails of ray-finned fishes, while others possessed a unique three-part fan structure.

The Dipnoi (lungfishes) were equipped with gills for breathing in the water and lungs for breathing air. The behavior of living species of lungfishes shows us that they can adapt to air breathing in times of stress, such as when their water becomes stagnant and low on oxygen, or during times of drought, when they cannot fully submerge. While these fish were not designed to live for long periods outside of the water, they may have been able to survive an extended drought by burying themselves in the mud and hibernating, as do their living, freshwater descendants in Africa. Evidence of lungfish burrows has been discovered in sediments dating from the Devonian Period. Some examples of such burrows dating from the Carboniferous Period include skeletal material from these fish.

All varieties of lobe-finned fishes appear to have been aggressive predators. Some may have been ambush predators that hovered in murky waters and lunged at passing prey with their large mouths. Most lobe-finned fishes had sharp teeth for grabbing and tearing prey, but lungfishes developed an alternative that consisted of dentine plates for crushing instead of pointed teeth. This kind of dental battery would have enabled the lungfish to eat hard foods such as shelled invertebrates.

Following is a guide to some of the most important species of lobe-finned fishes from the Paleozoic Era.

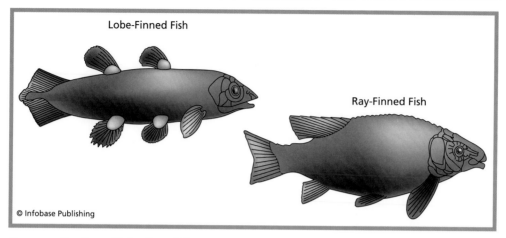

Lobe-Finned Fish

Ray-Finned Fish

© Infobase Publishing

Compare the fins of lobe-finned fishes and ray-finned fishes. The fins of lobe-finned fishes are more muscular and fanlike, which probably helped lobe-finned fishes hunt prey.

Porolepiformes

These early lobe-finned fishes existed only during the Devonian Period; they are found in marine and estuarine deposits in Scotland and North America. The porolepiforms had long bodies, short, broad heads with small eyes, and several rows of teeth on the lower jaw. Their scales varied from thick, rectangular types to larger, rounded ones in some of the later species.

The biting power of the porolepiform jaw was improved by a unique jointed skull. At the roof of the mouth, the skull was divided into front and back halves by a joint. When the animal bit down on its prey, more force was exerted by the downward-cleaving motion of the top and front part of the jaw. This was a necessary adaptation because the predominant prey of the porolepiforms may have been smaller ray-finned fishes with thick, protective scales.

A characteristic member of this clade of lobe-finned fishes was *Gyroptychius,* from the Middle Devonian of Scotland. Measuring about 12 inches (30 cm) long, *Gyroptychius* had small eyes, a short snout, and a long mouth. Its tail differed from those of later lobe-finned fishes in that it consisted of a simple, central bony spine with a triangular fringe on the top and bottom. The body of *Gyroptychius* was long, and all but its pectoral fins were positioned on the rear part of its torso.

Osteolepiformes

The osteolepiforms are the best evolutionary link between terrestrial vertebrates. The osteolepiforms had a more efficient arrangement of fins than the porolepiforms: The fins of the osteolepiforms were concentrated more toward the midpoint of the long body. An early clue to the evolution of tetrapods is also seen in the consolidation of anterior skull bones in the osteolepiforms. In more basal lobe-finned fishes and lungfishes, the bones of the snout were an unpatterned mosaic of many small bones. As seen in the osteolepiform called *Osteolepis*, these bones began to consolidate into a pattern seen in later vertebrates, particularly those on land. Descriptions of two important species of osteolepiforms follow.

Osteolepis. This fish was 8 inches (20 cm) long; it is found in the Middle Devonian strata of Antarctica, India, Iran, Latvia, and Scotland. *Osteolepis* had two large, posteriorly pointed dorsal fins and a downward pointed tail with a larger fin lobe on the underside of a bony spine. The scales of *Osteolepis* were square, and there is evidence of tiny nerve canals running throughout the fish's dermal covering. This matrix of nerves may have been able to sense vibrations in the water and alert *Osteolepis* to the presence of predators or prey.

Eusthenopteron. This large lobe-finned fish is a key player in the understanding of the origin of terrestrial vertebrates. Several intriguing anatomical features make *Eusthenopteron* an excellent intermediate in this important transition. Most importantly, the bones of Eusthenopteron's pectoral and pelvic fins include many of the important elements that would be needed by a walking creature, thus giving it ancestral arms and legs in the form of fins. Although there are gaps in the fossil record between *Eusthenopteron* and early land vertebrates, scientists continue to find transitional phases that illustrate the transition from fin to limb. Other features that unite *Eusthenopteron* with early land animals include the makeup of its teeth, the design of its spine, and the arrangement of bones in the front of its skull. Fossils of *Eusthenopteron* have been found in Late Devonian rocks of Scotland, Central Asia, and Canada. It was a large fish that measured up to 4 feet (1.2 m) long. Its tail consisted of three strong supports joined by two rayed membranes. Its long dorsal fins, pelvic fins, and anal fin were near the rear of the body; its strong pectoral fins were close to the head.

Actinistia (*Coelacanths*)

The actinistians include the coelacanths, living fishes with roots in the Middle Devonian. Some smaller, early species lived in freshwater habitats, but most coelacanths were large marine creatures that measured about 3 feet (1 m) long or more. Fossil species look virtually identical to living species. Coelacanths typically have short, broad bodies, large, fleshy fins, a tall skull, and a short snout. Their teeth are short and sharp. The tail is divided into a three-part structure that consists of a short, central support on the end of the fish's spinal column that is flanked by larger, feathery, fanlike lobes. The living genus of coelacanth is *Latimeria*. It has been found in the Indian Ocean in areas that range from Madagascar, off the coast of

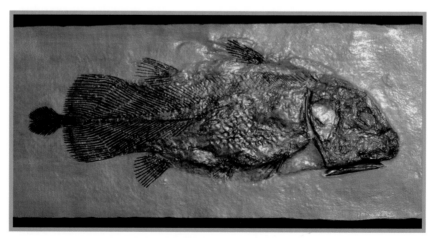

The *Latimeria* fossil is named in honor of Marjorie Courtenay-Latimer.

Africa, to Indonesia. Extinct species of actinistians from the Devonian Period include *Dictyonosteus* and *Diplocercides*.

Dipnoi

The lungfishes first appear in the fossil record of the Early Devonian Epoch. Three freshwater genera survive today, in Australia, Africa, and South America. Lungfishes have gills for breathing as well as a set of lungs. The swim bladder, used for buoyancy in most fishes, has been modified into a lung in the lungfishes. External nostrils, positioned low along the sides of the snout, are used by these fishes to breathe air. Unlike some other lobe-finned fishes, lungfishes did not have a jointed skull to improve their bite. The lungfish skull was solid, and the teeth were replaced by dentine-covered bumpy plates on the roof of the mouth and the lower jawbone. Among several known species of Paleozoic lungfish are *Dipterus* and *Griphognathus*.

Dipterus. *Dipterus* dates from the Middle to Late Devonian of Germany and Scotland. It was a lungfish of moderate size, measuring about 14 inches (35 cm) long. Its jaws display the robust crushing surface of dentine bumps that these fishes had instead of pointed teeth. The tail of *Dipterus* was short and only moderately frilled. The pectoral fins were long and narrow, with frills around their bony core. The pelvic, anal, and pectoral fins of *Dipterus* were situated close to the rear of the body. It had thick, rounded, overlapping scales. The endoskeleton of this fish was lighter and greatly reduced over those of earlier lungfishes, a trend that continued in the evolution of the Dipnoi.

Griphognathus. This lungfish is found in Late Devonian sediments of Australia and Germany. *Griphognathus* had several derived characteristics for a lungfish; these included a long, pointed snout; small, toothlike denticles lining its jaws; and a longer tail than *Dipterus*. Its gills were covered with muscular arches, the purpose of which may have been to break off pieces of coral that it could then grind with its small, rasping teeth.

(continues on page 154)

THINK ABOUT IT

The Coelacanth: A Living Fossil

Finding a living lobe-finned fish from the 360-million-year-old Actinistia (coelacanth) taxon seems about as likely as finding a living dinosaur in South America or a saber-toothed cat roaming central Europe. Yet that is exactly what South African naturalist Marjorie Courtenay-Latimer (1907–2004) found on the deck of a fishing trawler in 1938. Courtenay-Latimer was a naturalist and curator with the tiny East London Museum on the east coast of South Africa; she also was the friend of a fish expert named J.L.B. Smith (1897–1968) at Rhodes University College in Grahamstown, South Africa. Courtenay-Latimer routinely visited the docks to examine the hauls of fishing boats in search of a specimen or two for her museum. On one such visit, on December 23, 1938, a trawler's promising load of sharks caught her interest. As she examined the catch, Courtenay-Latimer saw something unusual. At the bottom of the pile of dead fish, poking out just enough for her to see, were the blue scaled fins of a large and "queer looking" fish. After the mangled body was pulled out of the pile, Courtenay-Latimer knew that she had found something truly strange. She hauled the heavy, smelly 127-pound (57 kg) fish to her museum to try to identify it. Unable to do so, she drew a sketch of her find and sent it off with a letter to J.L.B. Smith, a noted ichthyologist who had named many new species of fish. In the letter, Courtenay-Latimer described the fish as having "heavy scales, almost armour like, the fins resemble limbs, and are scaled right up to a fringe of filament. The spinous dorsal, has tiny white spines down each filament."

Smith did not receive Courtenay-Latimer's letter until after the Christmas holiday, but he was quick to reply with a cable message in which he declared, "MOST IMPORTANT PRESERVE SKELETON AND GILLS." He later said, "My surprise would have been little greater if I had seen a dinosaur walking down the street." By the time Smith replied, the inside organs of the fish had unfortunately been discarded; but the skin and skeleton remained in safekeeping until Smith arrived on February 16, 1939, to examine the fish. He knew from Courtenay-Latimer's sketch that she may have made the catch of the century, and he wasn't disappointed when he saw the specimen in person. Smith announced to the world that the coelacanth, once believed to have been extinct since the days of the dinosaurs, was indeed alive and well and living off the coast of Africa. "Though it was difficult to believe so incredible a thing," said Smith, "I identified the fish as a coelacanth and named it *Latimeria* in appreciation of what Miss Courtenay-Latimer had done."

First described in 1836 by Louis Agassiz, a Swiss naturalist (1807–1873), the coelacanth was known only from its fossils until this surprising catch in 1938. Although Smith hailed from a small college and Courtenay-Latimer, from a tiny, underfunded museum, the two knew an opportunity when they saw one. Determined to find additional specimens, Smith put out a request to local fishermen in the form of a wanted poster. "Look carefully at this fish," declared the poster. "It may bring you good fortune. Note the peculiar double tail, and the fins. . . . If you have the good fortune to catch or find one DO NOT CUT OR CLEAN IT IN ANY WAY but get it whole at once to a cold storage . . ." On the poster, Smith provided his address and offered a tidy sum of money for new specimens. Smith's efforts did not pay off until 1952, when a second specimen was caught. Since that time, more than 200 specimens have been caught in the Comoros Islands region of the Indian Ocean; and another **population** of *Latimeria* has been discovered in Indonesia, where the fish have been videotaped in their own habitat for the first time. The 1938 specimen is mounted and still resides in the East London Museum, where Marjorie Courtenay-Latimer once worked as curator.

The biology of *Latimeria* tells us much about the living habits of this ancient line of lobe-finned fishes. It is a large fish that measures up to 6 feet (1.8 m) long and weighs a robust 215 pounds (98 kg). Living species dwell at great depths that range from about 490 to 2,200 feet (150 to 700 m); some groups of coelacanths have been observed living in underwater caves at depths that average 650 feet (200 m). It is thought that these fish live to be 30 or 40 years old. Female *Latimeria* are larger than males. Based on the examination of the stomach contents of caught

(continues)

(continued)

specimens, *Latimeria* feeds primarily on fishes and soft-bodied invertebrates. Lantern fish, cardinal fish, eels, and even squid and octopus have been found in the stomachs of caught specimens. *Latimeria* is a drift feeder; it lurks with its head tipped downward, waiting for prey to swim by. It grabs prey with a quick movement of its jaws, grasps the hapless animal with its sharp, pointed teeth, and quickly gulps the victim down whole.

It was once thought that the coelacanths were closely related to the first land vertebrates (tetrapods). The discovery of *Latimeria* brought hope that the living coelacanth would provide direct information about the evolutionary transition from fish to tetrapods. The link between coelacanths and tetrapods has not turned out to be so close, however, given the anatomical and genetic differences that have been confirmed through close study of the living fish. *Latimeria* has no functional lungs, no internal nostrils, and no upper jawbones like those in tetrapods. These differences place the fish further down the evolutionary line of animals that led directly to land animals.

The diminishment of the coelacanth's link to land animals does nothing, however, to diminish what is perhaps an even more puzzling mystery: How did such a primitive group of fish remain virtually unchanged for more than 70 million years?

(continued from page 151)

VERTEBRATES EVOLVING IN TWO DIRECTIONS

The bony fishes occupy an unusual position in the history of life. By the end of the Paleozoic, these increasingly diverse creatures had established the supremacy of vertebrates in the world's oceans, lakes, and streams. With the passing of the Paleozoic Era, fishes were at the vanguard of an evolutionary trend that put vertebrates at the top of the food chain. It was the beginning of what J. John

Sepkoski called the time of Modern fauna and the domination of vertebrates for the foreseeable future. Fishes with jaws, and the bony fishes in particular, ruled the seas.

Bony fishes were also responsible for taking vertebrates in another direction entirely, from the water to the land. The roots of all land animals are found in the lineage of the lobe-finned fishes that adapted to life in near-shore and freshwater environments and eventually developed the ability to breathe, eat, reproduce, and move about on land as effectively as they had done in the water. It was a change that began in the oceans through small but incrementally significant modifications in the anatomy and physiology of fishes as they slowly extended their domain beyond the water.

SUMMARY

This chapter described the anatomical characteristics of the bony fishes and introduced prominent groups of these fishes that thrived during the Paleozoic Era.

1. The most numerous members of the jawed vertebrates are the *Osteichythes*, or bony fishes.

2. Osteichthyans were the first fishes with an endoskeleton composed of apatite bone instead of cartilage.

3. Osteichthyans are divided into two large groups: the Actinopterygii, or "ray fins," and the Sarcopterygii, or "lobe" or "fleshy fins."

4. *Psarolepis,* from the Late Silurian Epoch, is a fossil fish with a mosaic of features found in both jawless and jawed fishes. It was a basal ancestor to both the ray-finned fishes and the lobe-finned fishes.

5. Ray-finned fishes can be grouped according to their appearance in the fossil record, a reflection of the evolutionary history of the group. Early actinopterygians span the time from the Carboniferous Period to the Triassic Period; the neopterygians are rooted in the Late Permian Period but rose to prominence from the Triassic to the Jurassic Period; and the

teleosts, an offshoot of the neopterygians, span the time from the Jurassic Period to the present. The teleosts represent the most abundant fish group living today.

6. The early actinopterygian fishes adopted the successful arrangement of fins seen in the acanthodians and the placoderms that is still seen in most modern fishes.

7. Neopterygians improved on earlier ray-finned fishes through major changes to the jaws, the shape of the skull, and the tail.

8. Lobe-finned fishes—the sarcopterygians—arose during the Early Devonian Epoch and were an early group of bony fishes. One branch of the lobe-finned fishes included lungfishes.

9. Lobe-finned fishes, and specifically forms such as *Eusthenopteron,* were ancestors of the first land vertebrates.

CONCLUSION

The story of vertebrate evolution began in the Paleozoic seas with the development of fishes. The first fishes were defined, in great part, by the constraints of survival in the water. Fishes were among the first organisms to evolve a body plan optimized for effective swimming. These adaptations were born from the escalating needs of both predatory and prey creatures to become mobile and agile in the water. The resulting fish body plan has been fine-tuned many times over in the subsequent evolution of many different kinds of fishes.

The origin and evolution of the fishes was also influenced by fluctuating changes in Earth's habitats. The Paleozoic Era is recognized as the most geologically and climatically changeable span of the planet's history. The atmosphere, oceans, and lands of the Paleozoic went through several key formative stages. Dramatic changes in sea level, oxygen levels, and global temperature affected the existence of life time and time again and resulted in several major extinction events. With each extinction came renewed opportunities for remaining species to diversify and spread into Earth's changing habitats.

The family tree of all vertebrates began with the fishes. It branched out to terrestrial habitats by way of the lobe-finned fishes, several taxa of which were able to breathe outside of the water. These curious fishes, which are now considered rare and atypical members of the community of extant fishes, spawned the rise of an entirely new form of vertebrate—the land-dwelling tetrapod.

APPENDIX ONE:
GEOLOGIC TIME SCALE

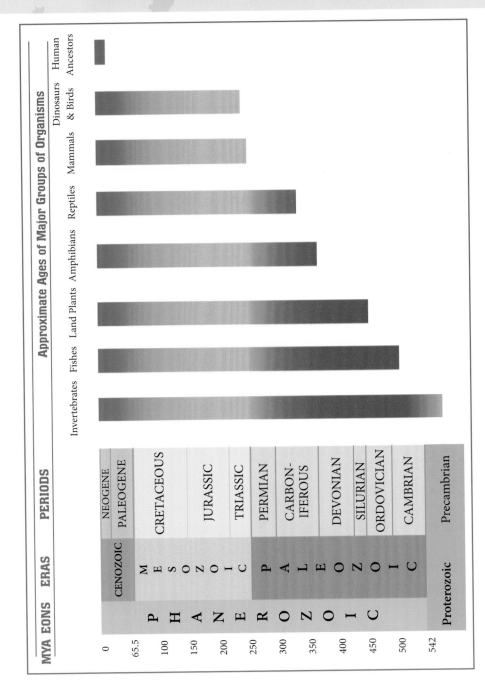

APPENDIX TWO: POSITIONAL TERMS

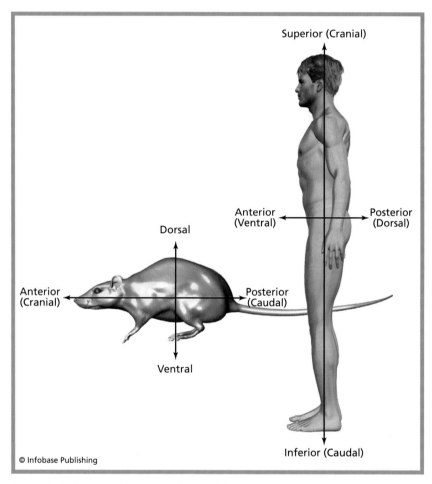

Positional terms used to describe vertebrate anatomy

GLOSSARY

absolute dating   A technique for determining the age of a rock by measuring the rates of decay of radioactive elements found in the rock; also called radiometric dating.

adaptation   Changes in a lineage of organisms in response to environmental stress.

Agnatha   Jawless fishes.

analogies   Similar traits that arise in organisms that are not related to one another.

anatomy   Term used to describe the basic biological systems of an animal, such as the skeletal and muscular systems.

annelids   (Annelida) Animal phylum whose members have a fluid-filled, segmented body, are worm-shaped, have a nervous system on the underside of the body, and possess at least one pair of hairlike bristles; annelids include worms that live on the land and in the sea, and leeches.

anoxia   Lack of oxygen; anoxia can causing suffocation; this condition can occur in the atmosphere or in a body of water such as the ocean.

anterior   Directional term indicating the head end of a vertebrate; also known as the cranial end.

apatite   One of the mineral ingredients of vertebrate bones; apatite is composed of calcium phosphate, a building block of cellular bone.

appendicular   Term used to describe limb elements of the vertebrate body.

arthropods   (Arthropoda) Animal phylum whose members have a segmented body, body regions dedicated to specific functions, a jointed exoskeleton, and a nervous system on the underside of the body; arthropods include trilobites, crabs, lobsters, brine shrimp, barnacles, insects, spiders, scorpions, and centipedes.

average global temperature   The combined average of air temperatures near the surface of land and sea.

axial   Lengthwise along the axis of the body, as in the direction of growth of the vertebrate skeleton.

background extinction   A background extinction may occur suddenly, or it may occur slowly over a long period of time; a background extinction usually affects only one species at a time.

Bacteria   One of the three domains of living organisms; it includes members of the kingdom Bacteria—single-celled organisms whose cells do not have a nucleus (prokarotes) and whose metabolism is oxygen based.

basal   At the base or earliest level of evolutionary development; a term usually used to refer to an ancestral taxon.

benthic   Term used to describe a stationary, seafloor-dwelling creature such as a sea squirt, tunicate, or ascidian.

bias   Word used to describe natural circumstances that favor fossilization, including the population, anatomy, size, and biology and habitat of a species.

bilateral symmetry   Form of symmetry in which one side of the body is a mirror image of the other.

Cambrian Period   Period of geologic time lasting from 488 million to 542 million years ago.

carbon-14 dating   A form of absolute dating based on the decay rate of the element carbon 14, which is taken in by living organisms from the air; once an animal dies, carbon 14 begins to decay.

cartilage   A noncalcified skeletal material; also called gristle; cartilage is the primary skeletal component of sharks and rays.

cast   A type of fossil made when a body mold from an organism is filled with another element; a cast can retain the outer shape and size of the organism.

caudal   Directional term indicating the tail end of a vertebrate; also known as the posterior.

cellular bone   Form of bone that lives and grows as tissue, has channels for blood vessels, and is made up of calcium phosphate; cellular bone is found in all vertebrates.

Cephalochordata   Eel-like members of a subphylum of chordates that lack skulls and backbones.

Chordata   Animal phylum whose members possess a notochord, a nerve cord that runs on top of the notochord, gill slits for breathing, and a tail; chordates include lancelets, salps, ascidians, and larvaceans.

clade   A group of related organisms that includes all the descendants of a single common ancestor.

cladistics   A way of classifying organisms by comparing their anatomical features; categorizing organisms because of their shared characteristics.

cladogram   A diagram used to illustrate the cladistic (evolutionary) relationships between groups of organisms.

climate   The kind of weather that occurs at a particular place over time.

cnidarians   (Cnidaria) Animal phylum whose members have a body consisting of a large central chamber that receives and digests food; includes corals, jellyfish, sea anemones, sea fans, sea pens, and the Portuguese man-of-war.

continental drift   The slow and gradual movement and transformation of the continents due to shifting of the tectonic plates of Earth's crust.

convergent evolution   Term used to describe a situation in which unrelated species each develop similar adaptations to similar environmental conditions.

coprolite   Fossilized animal feces.

core   A region at the center of the Earth; the core consists of a dense, solid inner core, at the center of the Earth, that floats within a surrounding liquid outer core.

cranial   Directional term indicating the head end of a vertebrate; also known as the anterior.

cross-cutting   The principle of cross-cutting states that any geologic feature is younger than anything else that it cuts across.

crust   The outer layer of the Earth, including both dry land and ocean floors.

dentine   The primary mineral component of teeth.

deposit feeder   Marine animal that eats by extracting nutrients from mud on the seafloor.

derived   Term used to describe a trait of an organism that is a departure from the most primitive, or basal, form.

dermal   Pertaining to the skin, as in dermal armor.

developmental   Pertaining to aspects of the reproduction and growth of organisms.

distal   Positional term indicating a part of the vertebrate body that is positioned toward the outside of the body.

DNA   (deoxyribonucleic acid) The molecule of life, which carries genetic instructions from parent to offspring.

domain   A taxononic level of classification higher than the kingdom; the domain was proposed in the 1970s by Carl Woese and George

Fox but not widely accepted until 1996; the three domains of life include Bacteria, Archaea, and Eukarya.

dorsal   Directional term indicating the back side of a vertebrate.

ecosystem   A population of all living organisms and the environment in which they live.

enamel   A crystalline covering of the crown of a tooth.

endoskeleton   An internal skeleton, usually consisting of bones, such as is found in vertebrates.

eon   One of the three longest spans of geologic time; the Archean ("ancient") Eon stretched from the earlierst Earth, 4.5 billion years ago, to 2.5 billion years ago; the Proterozoic ("early life") Eon began after the Archean and lasted from 2.5 billion to 542 million years ago; the Phanerozoic ("visible life") Eon began 542 million years ago and still goes on.

epicenter   The location on Earth's surface directly above the point of origin of an earthquake.

epoch   a span of geologic time ranking below the period; the Phanerozoic Eon is divided into three eras, 11 periods, and 34 epochs. The longest epoch is the Early Cretaceous Epoch, spanning 46 million years; the shortest is the Pridoli Epoch (in the Siluran Period), which spans only 2 million years. Epochs are sometimes broken down further into smaller divisions of time known as ages.

era   A span of geologic time ranking below the eon; the Archean Eon is divided into four eras dating from more than 4 billion years ago to 2.5 billion years ago; the Proterozoic Eon is divided into three eras dating from about 2.5 billion years ago to 542 million years ago; the ongoing Phanerozoic Eon is divided into three eras, the Paleozoic, the Mesozoic, and the Cenozoic; the Paleozoic ("ancient life") Era lasted from 542 million to 251 million years ago; the Mesozoic ("middle life") Era lasted from 251 million to 65 million years ago; the Cenozoic ("recent life") Era began 65 million years ago and continues to the present.

erosion   The removal and displacement of Earth's surface by the action of running water, rain, wind, glaciers, and ice sheets.

Eukarya   One of the three domains of living organisms; it includes for kingdoms—Protista, Fungi, Plantae, and Animalia—all of which consist of multicelled organisms with a distinct cell structure whose nucleus contains strands of DNA.

eukaryotes   Living organisms in the domain Eukarya; multicelled organisms with a distinct cell structure whose nucleus contains strands of DNA.

evaporate   To turn water into gas by heating it; sunlight evaporates water found in oceans, lakes, and streams.

evolution   The natural process that causes species to change gradually over time; evolution is controlled by changes to the genetic code—the DNA—of organisms.

exoskeleton   A skeleton that forms on the outside of the body, as in invertebrates such as anthropods.

extant   Term used to describe an organism that is living today.

extinction   The irreversible elimination of an entire species of plant or animal because the species cannot adapt effectively to changes in its environment.

fauna   Animals found in a given ecosystem.

feedback   System of natural processes in which chemical exchanges take place among seawater, the atmosphere, weathering rock, and the metabolic activity of organisms.

forelimb   One of the two front legs of a vertebrate.

fossil   Any physical trace of prehistoric life.

fossilization   The physical process by which the remains of an organism become a fossil.

gene   A microscopic unit on a DNA molecule that controls inherited traits.

genetics   The scientific study of DNA, genes, and inherited traits.

geologic timescale   A scale for measuring time based on observations about the layers of the Earth and how long these layers took to accumulate.

geophysics   A branch of geology that studies the composition and structure of Earth, its atmosphere, its oceans, and its magnetic fields based on the principles of physics.

glaciation   The formation of glaciers; glacier-making activity.

global chemostat   A complex, self-regulatory system by which the ocean naturally maintains its optimum chemical balance.

global heat budget   Ratio expressing the amount of global radiation that is absorbed or reflected by the Earth.

gnathostomes   ("jaw-mouthed") All vertebrates with jaws.

gradualism   Evolution through slow and gradual changes over a long period of time that lead to major biological changes to a species.

greenhouse effect   The trapping of reflected solar radiation by water vapor in clouds, ozone in the lower atmosphere, and atmospheric methane and carbon dioxide (CO_2) gas.

heterocercal   Term used to describe the tail of an aquatic vertebrate that is asymmetrical and in which the upper portion is larger than the lower portion; the upper portion is usually reinforced by a hard body part, such as the caudal end of the backbone.

hind limb   One of the two rear legs of a vertebrate.

homeostasis   The natural biological stability of a living organism.

homologies   Structural and behavioral traits that different species of organisms have inherited from a common ancestor.

hybrid   An offspring of two animals of different varieties, breeds, or species, such as a mule.

igneous rock   Rock that forms from the cooling of once-molten matter from the interior of the Earth.

impact crater   A crater in the crust of the Earth caused by the strike of an extraterrestrial body such as an asteroid or meteorite.

index fossils   Fossils that are widely distributed and easily recognized but that are restricted to certain geologic strata; these qualities make such fossils useful for dating related stratigraphic layers around the Earth.

kingdom   One of the six major hierarchical classifications of life at a taxonomic level just under domain; the six kingdoms are Archaebacteria, Bacteria, Protista, Fungi, Plantae, and Animalia.

long-term biological adaptation   A physiological change that occurs when an organism acclimates to long-term exposure to a new or changing environment; long-term biological adaptations are not passed on to offspring.

macrophagous   Word used to describe a predator or scavenger, a creature that preys on other organisms.

magma   Hot, liquid rock in Earth's mantle and crust; called lava when it comes to the surface through a volcanic eruption.

magnetometer   A scientific instrument that measures the strength of Earth's magnetic field.

mantle   A layer of the Earth that surrounds the core and lies between the core and the outer surface or crust.

mass extinction   An extinction event that kills off more than 25 percent of all species in a million years or less.

metabolism   The ability of a living organism to get energy and nutrients from the outside, convert outside energy and nutrients into its own energy, release waste, and grow.

metazoans   Multicelled organisms.

mineralization   A process of fossilization caused by water seepage through sediment containing the remains of an organism; over time, minerals carried by the water replace parts of the organism's skeleton.

mold   A type of fossil created when the body of an organism dissolves away, leaving a hollow impression of an original body part in the sedimentary rock.

molecular   Consisting of molecules; pertaining to the microscopic study of biological molecules.

molecular cladistics   In the classifying of organisms, a discipline that compares biological elements of different species at the molecular level; this discipline includes the study of genes and DNA.

morphological   Pertaining to the body form and structure of an organism.

mutations   Slight, unpredictable variations in the genetic code that happen when organisms reproduce.

natural selection   One of Charles Darwin's observations regarding the way evolution works; given the complex and changing conditions under which life exists, those individuals with the most favorable combination of inherited traits may survive and reproduce while others may not.

notochord   A stiff rod running along the back of an organism; found in members of the phylum Chordata.

oceanic ridge   Undersea mountain range.

onychophorans   (Onychophora) Animal phylum whose members possess 14 to 43 pairs of unjointed legs, a worm-shaped body, two antennae, appendages forming jaws around the mouth, and two more stubby appendages near the mouth; onychophorans include the velvet and "walking" worms.

organism   Any living plant, animal, bacterium, archaebacterium, protist, or fungus.

outer core   The layer of the Earth that surrounds the inner core; the outer core is liquid and is made up largely of iron and nickel; the inner core floats inside the outer core.

paleoclimatology   Study of prehistoric climates through geologic evidence.

paleontologist   A scientist who studies prehistoric life, often using fossils.

paraphyletic   Term used to describe a group of organisms that evolved from a common ancestor but that does not include all of the descendants of that ancestor.

period   A span of geologic time ranking below the era; the Phanerozoic Eon is divided into three eras and 11 periods, each covering a span of millions of years; the longest of these periods, including the three in the Mesozoic Era, are sometimes further broken down into smaller divisions of time.

pharynx   The connection between the mouth and the throat through which food and air pass.

photosynthesis   A metabolic process in which an organism's cells convert energy from the Sun, carbon dioxide, and water to reproduce their cells; the waste product of photosynthesis is free oxygen released into the atmosphere.

phyla   The major subdivisions of organisms after one of the three major kingdoms of life; the word *phyla* is the plural of *phylum*.

phylogeny   The history of the evolutionary relationships among species, which can be diagrammed; also known as the tree of life.

physiology   The way in which an animal's parts work together and are adapted to help the organism survive.

population   Members of the same species that live in a particular area.

posterior   Directional term indicating the tail end of a vertebrate; also known as the caudal end.

poriferans   (Porifera) Animal phylum whose members have cells that are not organized into tissues or organs; poripherans are composed primarily of chambers for channeling water; they include the sponges.

Precambrian   The unit of geologic time that lasted from the beginning of Earth, 4.5 billion years ago, until 542 million years ago.

precipitation   Rain or snow.

predation   Feeding on other live animals.

predator   An animal that actively seeks and feeds on other live animals.

prehistory   History of life on Earth prior to the written history of humans; prehistoric time.

proximal   Directional term used to indicate a part of a vertebrate that is closer to the center of the body of the animal.

punctuated equilibria   Rapid evolution of a given species followed by a long period in which little change occurs.

relative dating   Determining the date of one layer of the Earth by comparing it to a previously identified layer.

rift   In Earth's crust, a gap between two tectonic plates that have moved apart.

scavenger   An animal that feeds on the dead remains of other animals.

sedimentary rock   Rock that forms in layers from the debris of other rocks or the remains of organisms.

seismograph   A scientific instrument used to detect, measure, and record seismic waves caused by earthquakes, thereby creating a permanent record of Earth's motion.

self-organization   A mathematical basis for predicting the seemingly spontaneous occurrence of order, developed by Stuart Kauffman as an adjunct to the evolutionary theory of natural selection.

short-term biological adaptation   A temporary physiological change that occurs naturally in an organism when it encounters a change to its environment; short-term biological adaptations are not passed on to offspring.

sipunculans   (Sipuncula) Animal phylum whose members have a plump, peanut-shaped, unsegmented body with a long mouth appendage that can be retracted into the body; sipunculans' bodies are muscular, with a hard outer covering; they include burrowing marine worms.

small shelly fauna   Tiny marine animals from the Early Cambrian Epoch whose remains include fossils of the hard, shell-like body parts they left behind.

species   In classification, the most basic biological unit of living organisms; members of a species can interbreed and produce fertile offspring.

stromatolites   Near-shore, multilayered, rocklike structures created by photosynthesizing bacterial organisms that live in vast colonies in shallow ocean waters; fossil stromatolites represent one of the oldest known records of life.

subduction zone   A deep trench in the seafloor caused by the collision of tectonic plates.

superposition   The principle of superposition states that younger rocks are generally found on top of older rocks.

suspension feeder   Marine animal that catches, traps, and filters out food particles floating through the water.

taxon   A single unit of classification.

taxa   A group unit of classification.

taxonomy   The science of classifying living and extinct species of organisms.

tectonic plates   Large, slowly moving slabs of crust that ride on top of Earth's semiliquid and molten mantle.

tetrapods   Vertebrate animals with four limbs, or their evolutionary descendents that have modified or lost limbs; includes all amphibians, reptiles, mammals, and birds.

topography   The physical features of a place or habitat.

trace fossil   A type of fossil that preserves evidence of the presence of a prehistoric organism but that does not include body parts; fossilized trackways or feces are examples of trace fossils.

trackway   The fossilized footprints or markings left by a prehistoric animal.

transitional fossil   A fossil that represents intermediate conditions in the evolution of a species.

trilobite   An extinct form of arthropod whose fossils are found in rocks dating from the Early Cambrian to the Late Permian Epochs, with a three-part body and a hard exoskeleton.

uniformitarianism   A geologic principle originating with James Hutton; it states that the geologic forces that can be observed in the present are the same as the forces that shaped the Earth in the past.

Urochordata   A subphylum of chordates with bulbous, baglike bodies; the tadpolelike young have a notochord; a dorsal hollow nerve cord; and gill slits.

Vendian   Name assigned to a division of time, from 541 million to 630 million years ago, during which some of the earliest forms of multicelled animals lived.

Vendian fauna   Multicelled animals that lived during Vendian times, from 541 to 630 million years ago.

ventral   Directional term indicating the underside or belly of a vertebrate.

Vertebrata   Animals with backbones; the largest subphylum of chordates.

CHAPTER BIBLIOGRAPHY

Introduction

Wilford, John Noble, "When No One Read, Who Started to Write?" *The New York Times,* April, 6, 1999. Available online. URL: http://query.nytimes.com/gst/fullpage.html?res=9B01EFD61139F935A35757C0A9 6F958260. Accessed October 22, 2007.

Chapter 1 – Continents and Climates of the Paleozoic Era

Berner, Robert A. "Atmospheric Oxygen Over Phanerozoic Time." *Proceedings of the National Academy of Sciences of the United States of America* 96, no. 20 (September 28, 1999): 10955–10957

Chumakov, N.M. "Trends in Global Climate Changes Inferred from Geological Data." *Stratigraphy and Geological Correlation* 12, no. 2 (2004): 7–32.

DiMichele, William A., Hermann W. Pfefferkorn, and Robert A. Gastaldo. "Response of Late Carboniferous and Early Permian Plant Communities to Climate Change." *Annual Review of Earth and Planetary Sciences* 29 (May 2001): 461–487.

Dudley, Robert. "Atmospheric Oxygen, Giant Paleozoic Insects and The Evolution of Aerial Locomotor Performance." *Journal of Experimental Biology* 201 (1998): 1043–1050.

Goddéris, Yves, Louis M. François, and Ján Veizer. "The Early Paleozoic Carbon Cycle." *Earth and Planetary Science Letters* no. 190 (2001): 181–196.

Jacobs, David K., and David R. Lindberg. "Oxygen and Evolutionary Patterns in the Sea: Onshore/Offshore Trends and Recent Recruitment of Deep-Sea Faunas." *Proceedings of the National Academy of Sciences of the United States of America* 95 (August 1998): 9396–9401.

Kious, W. Jacquelyne, and Robert I. Tilling. *This Dynamic Earth: The Story of Plate Tectonics.* Washington, D.C.: The United States Geological Survey, 2001.

Palmer, Douglas. *Atlas of the Prehistoric World*. New York: Discovery Books, 1999.

Plummer, Charles C., David McGeary, and Diane H. Carlson. *Physical Geology*. New York: McGraw-Hill, 2005.

Prothero, Donald R., and Robert H. Dott Jr. *Evolution of the Earth*. New York: McGraw-Hill, 2004.

Saltzman, Barry. *Dynamical Paleoclimatology: Generalized Theory of Global Climate Change*. New York: Academic Press, 2002.

United States Geological Survey. "Inside the Earth." Available online. URL: http://pubs.usgs.gov/publications/text/inside.html. Accessed October 22, 2007.

University of California Museum of Paleontology. "Plate Tectonics: The Mechanism." Available online. URL: http://www.ucmp.berkeley.edu/geology/tecmech.html. Accessed October 22, 2007.

Wilf, Peter. "When Are Leaves Good Thermometers? A New Case for Leaf Margin Analysis." *Paleobiology* 23, no. 3 (1997): 373–390.

Chapter 2 – Paleozoic Mass Extinctions

DiMichele, William A., Hermann W. Pfefferkorn, and Robert A. Gastaldo. "Response of Late Carboniferous and Early Permian Plant Communities to Climate Change." *Annual Review of Earth and Planetary Sciences* 29 (May 2001): 461–487.

Ellis, Richard. *No Turning Back: The Life and Death of Animal Species*. New York: Harper Collins, 2004.

Flessa, Karl W., and David Jablonski. "Declining Phanerozoic background extinction rates: Effect of taxonomic structure?" *Nature,* January 17, 1985, 216–218.

Jin, Y.G., Y. Wang, W. Wang, Q.H. Shang, C.Q. Cao, and D.H. Erwin. "Pattern of Marine Mass Extinction Near the Permian-Triassic Boundary in South China," *Science,* July 21, 2000, 432–436.

Kirschvink, Joseph L., and Timothy D. Raub. "A Methane Fuse for the Cambrian Explosion: Carbon Cycles and True Polar Wander." *Comptes Rendus Geoscience* 335 (2003): 65–78.

Norman, David. *Prehistoric Life: The Rise of the Vertebrates*. New York: Macmillan, 1994.

Raup, David M. *Extinction: Bad Genes or Bad Luck?* New York: W.W. Norton, 1991.

———. *The Nemesis Affair*. New York: W.W. Norton, 1986.

Chapter 3 – Vertebrate Traits

Miller, Arnold I. "Memorial: J. John Sepkoski Jr.: A Personal Reflection." *Journal of Paleontology* (September 1999).

Prothero, Donald R., and Robert H. Dott Jr. *Evolution of the Earth*. New York: McGraw-Hill, 2004.

Sepkoski, J. John Jr., Richard K. Bambach, David M. Raup, and James W. Valentine. "Phanerozoic Marine Diversity and the Fossil Record," *Nature*, October 8, 1981, 435–437

Chapter 4 – Vertebrate Origins

Benton, Michael J. "Conodonts Classified at Last," *Nature*, February 5, 1987, 482–483.

Briggs, Derek, and Peter R. Crowther, eds. *Palaeobiology II*. London: Blackwell Publishing, 2004.

Chen, Jun-Yuan, Di-Ying Huang, and Chia-Wei Li. "An Early Cambrian Craniatelike Chordate," *Nature*, 1999, 518–522.

Donovan, S.K., and Paul, C.R.C., eds. *The Adequacy of the Fossil Record*. New York: John Wiley, 1998.

Fortey, Richard. *Life: A Natural History of the First Four Billion Years of Life on Earth*. New York: Alfred A. Knopf, 1998.

Gabbott, S.E., R.J. Aldridge, and J.N. Theron. "A Giant Conodont with Preserved Muscle Tissue from the Upper Ordovician of South Africa," *Nature*, April 27, 2002, 800–803.

Higgins, Alan. "Carboniferous Fossils: The Conodont Animal," *Nature*, March 10, 1983, 107–107.

Hou, Xian-Guang, Richard J. Aldridge, David J. Siveter, Derek J. Siveter, and Feng Xiang-Hong. "New Evidence on the Anatomy and Phylogeny of the Earliest Vertebrates." *Proceedings of the Royal Society of London* 269 (2002): 1865–1869.

Hou, Xian-Guang, Richard J. Aldridge, Jan Bergstrom, David J. Siveter, Derek J. Siveter, and Xiang-Hong Feng. *The Cambrian Fossils of Chengjiang, China: The Flowering of Early Animal Life*. London: Blackwell Publishing, 2004.

Morris, Simon Conway. *The Crucible of Creation: The Burgess Shale and the Rise of Animals*. Oxford: Oxford University Press, 1998.

Norman, David. *Prehistoric Life: The Rise of the Vertebrates*. New York: Macmillan, 1994.

Pechenik, Jan A. *Biology of the Invertebrates.* 5th ed. New York: McGraw-Hill, 2005.

Purnell, Mark A., Philip C.J. Donoghue, and Richard J. Aldridge. "Orientation and Anatomical Notation in Conodonts." *Journal of Paleontology* 74–1 (2000): 113–122.

Shu, D.-G., S. Conway Morris, J. Han, Z.-F. Zhang, K. Yasui, P. Janvier, L. Chen, X.-L. Zhang, J.-N. Liu, Y. Li, and H.-Q. Liu. "Head and backbone of the Early Cambrian vertebrate *Haikouichthys,*" *Nature,* January 30, 2003, 526–529.

Shu, Degan, and Simon Conway Morris. "Response to Comment on 'A New Species of Yunnanozoan with Implications for Deuterostome Evolution,'" *Science* May 30, 2003, 1372.

Young, Gavin C., Valya N. Karatajute-Talimaa, and Moya M. Smith. "A Possible Late Cambrian Vertebrate from Australia," *Nature,* October 31, 1996, 810–812.

Zhang, Shunxin, and Christopher R. Barnes. "*Anticostiodus,* a New Multielement Conodont Genus from the Lower Silurian, Anticosti Island, Quebec." *Journal of Paleontology* 74 (July 2000): 662–669.

Chapter 5 – Jawless Fishes

Fortey, Richard. *Life: A Natural History of the First Four Billion Years of Life on Earth.* New York: Alfred A. Knopf, 1998.

Hou, Xian-Guang, Richard J. Aldridge, David J. Siveter, Derek J. Siveter, and Feng Xiang-Hong. "New Evidence on the Anatomy and Phylogeny of the Earliest Vertebrates." *Proceedings of the Royal Society of London* 269 (2002): 1865–1869.

Hou, Xian-Guang, Richard J. Aldridge, Jan Bergstrom, David J. Siveter, Derek J. Siveter, and Xiang-Hong Feng. *The Cambrian Fossils of Chengjiang, China: The Flowering of Early Animal Life.* London: Blackwell Publishing, 2004.

Monastersky, R. "Waking Up to the Dawn of Vertebrates." *Science News* 156, no. 19 (November 6, 1999): 292.

Norman, David. *Prehistoric Life: The Rise of the Vertebrates.* New York: Macmillan, 1994.

Prothero, Donald R., and Robert H. Dott Jr. *Evolution of the Earth.* New York: McGraw-Hill, 2004.

Raven, Peter H., George B. Johnson, Jonathan B. Losos, and Susan R. Singer. *Biology.* 7th ed. New York: McGraw-Hill, 2005.

Sansom, Ivan J., Philip C.J. Donoghue, and Guillermo Albanesi. "Histology and Affinity of the Earliest Armoured Vertebrate." *Biology Letters* 1, no. 4 (December 22, 2005): 446–449.

Chapter 6 – Vertebrate Innovations

Fortey, Richard. *Life: A Natural History of the First Four Billion Years of Life on Earth.* New York: Alfred A. Knopf, 1998.

Kowalewski, Michal, and Patricia H. Kelley, eds. *The Fossil Record of Predation: Methods, Patterns, and Processes.* Paleontological Society Special Papers 8 (2002): 395–398.

Miller, Stephen A., and John P. Harley. *Zoology, Sixth Edition.* New York: McGraw-Hill, 2005.

Prothero, Donald R., and Robert H. Dott Jr. *Evolution of the Earth.* New York: McGraw-Hill, 2004.

Raven, Peter H., George B. Johnson, Jonathan B. Losos, and Susan R. Singer. *Biology, Seventh Edition.* New York: McGraw-Hill, 2005.

Shimeld, Sebastian M., and Peter W.H. Holland. "Vertebrate innovations." *Proceedings of the National Academy of Sciences of the United States of America* 97, no. 9 (April 25, 2000): 4449–4452.

Chapter 7 – Cartilaginous Fishes: The Sharks and Rays

Coates, M.I., and S.E.K. Sequeira, "A New Stethacanthid Chondrichthyan from the Lower Carboniferous of Bearsden, Scotland." *Journal of Vertebrate Paleontology* 21, no. 3 (2001): 438–459.

Coates, M.I., S.E.K. Sequeira, I.J. Sansom, and M.M. Smith. "Spines and Tissues of Ancient Sharks," *Nature*, December, 24/31, 1998: 729–730.

Eastman, C.R. "Karpinsky's Genus *Helicoprion*." *American Naturalist* 34, no. 403 (July 1900): 579–582.

———. "The Literature of *Edestus*." *American Naturalist* 39, no. 462 (June 1905): 405–409.

Ellis, Richard. "The Helicoprion Mystery: Where on ancient shark's body were its teeth located?" (brief article). *Natural History* (March 2001). Available online. URL: http://www.findarticles.com/p/articles/mi_m1134/is_2_110/ai_71317744. Accessed October 22, 2007

Kriwet, Jürgen. "Neoselachian remains (Chondrichthyes, Elasmobranchii) from the Middle Jurassic of SW Germany and NW Poland." *Acta Palaeontol. Pol.* 48, no. 4 (2003): 583–594

Larson, E. Richard, and James B. Scott. "Helicoprion from Elko County, Nevada." *Journal of Paleontology* 29, no. 5 (September, 1955): 918–919.

Maisey, John G., and M. Eric Anderson. "A Primitive Chondrichthyan Braincase from the Early Devonian of South Africa." *Journal of Vertebrate Paleontology* 21, no. 4 (2001): 702–713.

Maisey, John G. "Braincase of the Upper Devonian Shark *Cladodoides Wildungensis* (Chondrichthyes, Elasmobranchii), with Observations on the Braincase in Early Chondrichthyans." *Bulletin of the American Museum of Natural History* no. 288 (March 2, 2005): 1–103.

Markey, Sean. "World's Oldest Shark Fossil Found," *National Geographic News*, October 1, 2003. Available online. URL: http://news.nationalgeographic.com/news/2003/10/1001_031001_sharkfossil.html. Accessed October 22, 2007.

Miller, Randall F., Richard Cloutier, and Susan Turner. "The Oldest Articulated Chondrichthyan From the Early Devonian Period," *Nature*, October 2, 2003, 501–504.

Norman, David. *Prehistoric Life: The Rise of the Vertebrates.* New York: Macmillan, 1994.

Palmer, Douglas. *Atlas of the Prehistoric World.* New York: Discovery Books, 1999.

Prothero, Donald R., and Robert H. Dott Jr. *Evolution of the Earth.* New York: McGraw-Hill, 2004.

Rasmussen, Ann-Sofie, and Ulfur Arnason. "Molecular studies suggest that cartilaginous fishes have a terminal position in the piscine tree." *Proceedings of the National Academy of Sciences of the United States of America* 96 (March 1999): 2177–2182.

Sour-Tovar, Francisco, Sara A. Quiroz-Barroso, and Shelton P. Applegate. "Presence of Helicoprion (Chondrichthyes, Elasmobranchii) in The Permian Patlanoaya Formation, Puebla, Mexico." *Journal of Paleontology* 74, no. 2 (March 2000): 363–366.

Tiiu, Märss, and Gagnier, Pierre-Yves. "A New Chondrichthyan from the Wenlock, Lower Silurian, of Baillie-Hamilton Island, the Canadian Arctic." *Journal of Vertebrate Paleontology* 21, no. 4 (2001): 693–701.

Chapter 8 – Bony Fishes

Campbell, K.S.W., and R.E. Barwick. "A New Species of the Devonian Lungfish *Dipnorhynchus* from Wee Jasper, New South Wales." *Records of the Australian Museum* 51 (1999): 123–140.

Gould, Stephen Jay, ed. *The Book of Life.* New York: W.W. Norton, 1993.

Lund, Richard. "The New Actinopterygian Order Guildayichthyiformes from the Lower Carboniferous of Montana (USA)." *Geodiversitas* 22, no. 2 (2000): 171–206.

Miller, Stephen A., and John P. Harley. *Zoology.* 6th ed. New York: McGraw-Hill, 2005.

Norman, David. *Prehistoric Life: The Rise of the Vertebrates.* New York: Macmillan, 1994.

Trewin, N.H., and R.G. Davidson. "Lake-Level Changes, Sedimentation and Faunas in a Middle Devonian Basin-Margin Fish Bed." *Journal of the Geological Society*, 156, no. 3 (May 1999): 535–548.

FURTHER READING

Benton, Michael. *Vertebrate Paleontology*. 3rd ed. Oxford: Blackwell Publishing, 2005.

Fortey, Richard. *Life: A Natural History of the First Four Billion Years of Life on Earth*. New York: Alfred A. Knopf, 1998.

Gould, Stephen J., ed. *The Book of Life*. New York: W.W. Norton, 1993.

International Commission on Stratigraphy. "International Stratigraphic Chart" [Time Scale Chart]. Available online. URL: http://www.stratigraphy.org/.

Lambert, David. *Encyclopedia of Prehistory*. New York: Facts on File, 2002.

Morris, Simon Conway. *The Crucible of Creation: The Burgess Shale and the Rise of Animals*. Oxford: Oxford University Press, 1998.

Norman, David. *Prehistoric Life: The Rise of the Vertebrates*. New York: Macmillan, 1994.

Palmer, Douglas. *Atlas of the Prehistoric World*. New York: Discovery Books, 1999.

Prothero, Donald R., and Robert H. Dott, Jr. *Evolution of the Earth*. New York: McGraw-Hill, 2004.

Raven, Peter H., George B. Johnson, Jonathan B. Losos, and Susan R. Singer. *Biology*. 7th ed. New York: McGraw-Hill, 2005.

Taylor, Barbara. *Earth Explained: A Beginner's Guide to Our Planet*. New York: Henry Holt, 1997.

Troll, Ray. *Rapture of the Deep*. Berkeley: University of California Press, 2004.

Woese, Carl R. "Prokaryote Systematics: The Evolution of a Science." *Prokaryotes*, second edition, New York, Springer, 1990.

Xian-Guang Hou, Richard J. Aldridge, Jan Bergstrom, David J. Siveter, Derek J. Siveter, and Xiang-Hong Feng, *The Cambrian Fossils of Chengjiang, China: The Flowering of Early Animal Life*. London: Blackwell Publishing, 2004.

Web Sites

American Geological Institute: Constructing Understandings of Earth Systems

This site is an interactive reference, provided by the American Geological Institute, to the primary systems that work together to make the world we know, including the geosphere, the hydrosphere, the atmosphere, and the biosphere.

http://www.agiweb.org/education/cues/index.html

American Museum of Natural History: Life Forms

The American Museum of Natural History provides a guide to deep-sea hydrothermal animals, some of the most unusual and primitive creatures on the planet.

http://www.amnh.org/nationalcenter/expeditions/blacksmokers/life_forms.html

Australian Museum: Palaeontology

Exhibits on the site include Australia's Lost Kingdoms, a photographic journey that explores early fossils and life-forms found in Australia.

http://www.austmus.gov.au/palaeontology/index.htm

Hamlin, Jerome. The Fish Out of Time

This Web site includes video footage of live coelacanths in their natural habitat.

http://www.dinofish.com/

Kazlev, Alan, and Augustus White. Palaeos: The Trace of Life on Earth

This site is a robust and growing reference about all kinds of life-forms.

http://www.palaeos.com/

Lapworth Museum, University of Birmingham. Palaeontological Collections: Vertebrate Collection

Online exhibits explore early vertebrate life, particularly fishes, from the United Kingdom.

http://www.lapworth.bham.ac.uk/collections/palaeontology/vertebrates.htm

Maddison, D.R., and K.-S. Schulz. The Tree of Life Web Project

This site is hosted by the University of Arizona College of Agriculture and Life Sciences and the University of Arizona Library and provides a meticulously designed view of life-forms based on their phylogenetic (evolutionary) connections.

http://tolweb.org/tree/phylogeny.html

Paleontology Portal: Vertebrates

This site explores early vertebrate life; produced by the University of California Museum of Paleontology, the Paleontological Society, the Society of Vertebrate Paleontology, and the United States Geological Survey.

http://www.paleoportal.org/index.php?globalnav=fossil_gallery &sectionnav=taxon&taxon_id=16

Peripatus, Chris: Paleontology Page

Provides a privately compiled but exhaustive resource on many paleontology subjects, including a valuable look at the Burgess Shale fossils.

http://www.peripatus.gen.nz/Paleontology/Index.html

Public Broadcasting Service: Evolution Library: Evidence for Evolution

This resource outlines the extensive evidence in support of both the fact and the theory of evolution; the site's approach is based on studies of the fossil record, molecular sequences, and comparative anatomy.

http://www.pbs.org/wgbh/evolution/library/04/

Scotese, Christopher R.: Paleomap Project

This site is a valuable source of continental maps showing the positioning of the Earth's continents over the course of geologic time.

http://www.scotese.com/

Smithsonian National Museum of Natural History, Department of Paleobiology: Burgess Shale Fossil Specimens

A catalog of Burgess Shale fossil specimens, life depictions, and facts are listed on this site.

http://paleobiology.si.edu/burgess/burgessSpecimens.html#

United States Geological Survey. Inside the Earth

This site includes cutaway views of the composition of the Earth.

http://pubs.usgs.gov/publications/text/inside.html

University of California Museum of Paleontology: Fossil Evidence: Transitional Forms

This site gives a tutorial about transitional forms in the fossil record with illustrated examples.

http://evolution.berkeley.edu/evosite/lines/IAtransitional.shtml

Zwicker, Ken, and TERC: How Diverse Is Life on Your Site? Taxonomy and the Five Kingdoms of Life

An introduction to the taxonomy and systematics of the kingdoms of life can be found at this site.

http://www.concord.org/~btinker/guide/fieldguide/taxonomy. html

PICTURE CREDITS

INDEX

About the Author

THOM HOLMES is a writer specializing in natural history subjects and dinosaurs. He is noted for his expertise on the early history of dinosaur science in America. He was the publications director of *The Dinosaur Society* for five years (1991–1997) and the editor of its newsletter, *Dino Times*, the world's only monthly publication devoted to news about dinosaur discoveries. It was through the Society and his work with the Academy of Natural Sciences in Philadelphia that Thom developed widespread contacts and working relationships with paleontologists and paleo-artists throughout the world.

Thom's published works include *Fossil Feud: The Rivalry of America's First Dinosaur Hunters* (Silver Burdett Press, September 1997); *The Dinosaur Library* (Enslow, 2001–2002); *Duel of the Dinosaur Hunters* (Pearson Education, 2002); and *Fossil Feud: The First American Dinosaur Hunters* (Silver Burdett/Julian Messner, 1997). His many honors and awards include the National Science Teachers Association's *Outstanding Science Book of 1998,* Voices of Youth Advocates' 1997 Nonfiction Honor List, an Orbis Pictus Honor, and the Chicago Public Library Association's *"Best of the Best"* in science books for young people.

Thom did undergraduate work in geology and studied paleontology through his role as a staff educator with the Academy of Natural Sciences in Philadelphia. He is a regular participant in field exploration, including two recent expeditions to Patagonia in association with Canadian, American, and Argentinian institutions.